The Ghost Behind the Wheelchair

By

Lila Ridings Darnell

ISBN: 1-4033-1588-4 (ebook)
ISBN: 1-4033-1589-2 (Paperback)

This book is printed on acid free paper.

1stBooks - rev. 9/25/02

CHAPTER ONE

The Midnight Caller

I try not to see him but his shadow crosses my mind. He visits me in dreams, teasing with visions of the past or impossible hopes for the future.

I first noticed him in October 1991. He'd been there since the end of June, but there were other events and situations occupying my mind. The ghost was REAL, as was the new person then in my life. The ghost arrogantly stands just behind my quadriplegic son. In 1997, we are less aware of his presence.

Most importantly I would touch you with my story about this ghost and what he has left behind for us to learn. Since Scott's accident, I have met so many victims of paralysis and their parents, brothers, sisters, friends. NEVER would I choose this lesson; but having had it placed before us in no small or gentle way, we have also been given the opportunity to meet the most wonderfully brave, determined people that one could ever hope to become acquainted with. Those who must endure the injury come in all shapes and sizes and degrees of injury. Those of us who can really only watch and be there...for whatever...also come in all shapes and sizes and types.

I was so very, very fortunate and blessed during the time when this tragedy struck me and mine. Family, friends, new friends from work and in other environments who had previously been total strangers. People and experiences as "foreign" as the most distant alien could ever be became as close as the most intimate family members had been.

Robin, Michael and Robert were the first "new friends." Each played their own separate role. Robin was the counselor who involved me in the support group, the manuals and informational resources available, and who introduced me to Michael and the outstanding resources available in Orlando. Michael, another victim of spinal cord injury, just a year older than my son and whose injury was almost identical (level), and who was injured about 6 weeks before Scott's accident: Michael and I were in Orlando; Scott was in Missouri. Hell Week in Chesterfield lasted a week; then I had to return to Orlando where I would work three weeks, then return to spend a week in Missouri with Scott (Chesterfield first, then St. Louis later). During the three weeks away from Scott, I would spend time with Michael. At first, it was to help me learn…but also, I was hoping while I was spending time with Michael in Orlando, someone was doing likewise with Scott in Chesterfield, then St. Louis. In truth, Scott had Rachel and much, much family. I told myself and Scott that by going away, I was giving him my confidence that we'd get through this. The mother in me was so torn…How could I stay? How could I leave? If I didn't keep my job and my life together, how could I help Scott in the days ahead…? But how could I leave him? Answer: I had to…but only until I could come back. My youngest son, Roger, Scott's brother, gave me the answers. So while away, I spent time with Michael, and we became real friends. I still do but less than during those first two-three years. Five years later, unbelievable at the time, it seems life does have a way of going on, filling up again…for both the victims and for those who love the ones who have been injured.

AND…Robert, who called this stranger and told me about his life as a quadriplegic; who patiently answered my insensitive (I'm sure as I think back) questions. Robert is also about Scott's age and again, comparable level of injury. One learns about the "levels" and complete vs. incomplete. Robert was living alone! My mind was thinking it could happen; but it was just a hope until I talked with Robert and heard what he was doing, how he was living (driving a van, going to college; he had a dog and he seemed well-balanced emotionally, strong, confident, happy). Thank you forever after, dear Robert…only later did I come to realize how hard (in one respect) it is to go back and think how one does…try to explain it to others, advise, comfort. Life is full of getting on with it…to go back and remember takes a special strength, a generosity of spirit that should be bottled and sold to every depressed, discouraged, lonely and lost person in the world! From another point of view though, those who have been there KNOW the difference their support and advisements can make…having received so much from others during their own past, personal Hell Week and the weeks that followed, they hunger to return what has been so important to them. They no longer have such a huge need; others do and they more than anyone else can help.

How can the counselor or the doctor or the nurse stand before the newly paralyzed person and comfort them? How can a mother or father or brother or sister, husband or wife do any different? None of us who walk into the room can give the one in the bed or the wheelchair or the halo jacket much reassurance. Those in a peer group who have shared such an experience and reality can be heard more clearly by the one who so needs to listen and to hear that, "it will be all right; see, I've been where you are, look at me now."

Apart from an involvement with these three special people, I read everything I could get my hands on until my brain was saturated, couldn't absorb more. I read about dysreflexia, bladder programs, bowel programs, accessibility, skin care. I didn't read about TRANSFERS...and no one had really talked about "transfers." Of course there would need to be "transfers" but my mind had just been focused on Scott's staying alive...then, learning HOW to do EVERYTHING...One second I had a strong, totally athletic and independent 6'5" handsome firstborn; the next I had a fragile, totally dependent 6'5" handsome firstborn with a metal thing screwed into his head that had weights hanging down behind the bed. I kept asking how he was "feeling"; he couldn't FEEL...all of us ignorant others; the "old words" weren't applicable anymore and we hadn't learned the new ones yet.

Hell Week began for Scott on June 29, 1991; for me, shortly after midnight so June 30th. My brother, Bud, in Illinois called me. The day had been wonderful, spent with friends Billie & Steve; Billie and I had gone yard sale-ing while Steve so kindly trimmed my hedge along the driveway for me. I had been to Illinois and visited with Scott, met his new girlfriend Rachel, spent time with my mother about a month before, over the Memorial Day holiday. I'd just written my sister-in-law, Dot, in Oklahoma that I thought I could finally stop worrying about Scott. It seemed his life was more settled and positive than it had ever been before. Scott had always done EVERYTHING and done it all WELL...which was good and filled this mother's heart often with much pride, but it often bothered me that he would change plans, locations, hopes and dreams so often. I felt after that visit that he had calmed down and was ready to plan reasonably and long term; that he was content in life. I was so happy to see him in that frame of mind. He came out and worked on his truck...or boat...or something...under the tree in Mom's front yard. It was a simple visit but so pleasant. Our discussion was filled with harmony. We were on the same track and that was so reassuring; often, in times past, we hadn't been.

I went to bed that night with all those good thoughts on my mind; I had on the pajamas Scott had brought me from Pakistan, where he had worked for some duration...but I could not go to sleep. When the phone rang shortly after midnight, I was wide awake and had been punching my pillow, trying to find a special "go to sleep" mode. I had thought when Scott went to Pakistan, he was much too far away from this Mama. After this call, Chesterfield, Missouri, might as well have been as far away as Pakistan...It seemed an eternity getting there, as the extreme need to do so quickly was being realized.

Scott had been our star athlete...as graceful as a ballerina on all the ball fields: baseball, softball, football, basketball...He was never "reckless" but things kept happening to him. He wouldn't listen about being more careful; he'd hurt his back and had surgery and still was insistent about getting on full speed ahead with life. He had come into the world in a hurry and had never stopped. There were always more things, more places, more people to see, do…He'd permanently damaged his front teeth and broke his arm in a motorcycle accident when he was younger; he'd broken his leg in a football game on his 16th birthday; he was often injuring his ankles playing basketball…then, there had been two surgeries on his lower back while working on construction projects with his dad. I wasn't always patient or understanding. Too many things were beyond my control; it was frustrating only being involved in the hurting part and never the part that might keep things from happening in the first place; but then, so goes life and the experiences of parenting.

My first reaction when Bud called was that Scott had just been careless again…but I very shortly called Bud back and asked…how bad…? Walk? The terror arrived and grew with the answers. Scott had dived into shallow water and was being taken by helicopter from the small hospital in Greenville, Illinois, to St. Lukes West in Chesterfield, Missouri, as we spoke. The accident had happened hours earlier…I hadn't known what was happening until after midnight, in the middle of what proved to be an endless night.

I called the hospital in Chesterfield; Scott wasn't there yet but his father was. I talked briefly to Jim. I called my nephew, Joel, who was so close to Scott and had been with him at the lake. I called my sister, then remembered she was out of the state. I called the airline and made a reservation for the "earliest" flight out…which wasn't until about 6 or 6:30 the next morning. I tried calling Roger and Beth, his girlfriend. There had been a wedding reception for friends; they weren't in yet…I kept calling and leaving messages. The last message I left, I had talked with Jim again; and he had said there was danger that the swelling in Scott's neck might possibly shut down his automatic reflexes, that he might just stop breathing and die; so there was minimal control when I called Roger that last time. I was alone, it was the middle of the night and I was getting more and more scared with each passing minute. My son might be dying far away from me, and I couldn't get to him…

I called friends: Louise, Billie…I called Chuck and Mel from work to tell them my son had been hurt in a diving accident and I had to go to Illinois…I kept trying to get hold of Roger. I paid bills, I did anything and everything I could "think" to do just to get through one minute at a time…until I could at least get on the plane and on my way, praying that Scott was still alive this minute, now this one…and another.

Roger, like myself when he "heard," thought Scott had just done something careless again. Our initial conversation was short, and I didn't persist; I remembered my own reaction. Within a minimal amount of time…Roger called me back, ready to hear the reality of the situation. He and Beth then immediately came out to stay with me until I could leave. We made our plans, as we could. They would take me to the airport; then Roger would drive up as soon as he tended to a few things at home. We've been so "together" in this from that initial meeting that it's hard now to think we didn't "go up" together…and

7

it's painful knowing how awful that long drive had to have been for Roger, alone. At the time, I was so full of fear for Scott, my mind wasn't with Roger on the road during those long hours and over those agonizing miles. Both my sons have shown supreme strengths in the days, weeks and months that followed the accident, and there remains a dedicated pride that was fully born and acknowledged during Hell Week. We all just did what we had to do as it was needed. We had no way of knowing what those needs would be; we knew nothing of paralysis. Back then, our vocabulary did not include complete or incomplete, bowel programs, caths or supra pubics, transfers, or levels of injury as relate to spinal cord injuries. Quadriplegia meant immobility; no active life or involvement; complete dependence.

When I was first HIT with the realization of the crisis we were in that late night/early morning, my only source of comfort was God's Word…that He would not give us more than we had strength to bear.

Roger took me to the airport early the next morning around 5:30 a.m., well before I could board the plane and get started. It was so empty and quiet…I couldn't stand the emptiness. God Bless my friend, Louise, and her gift of gab! I called and talked to her until my plane was ready to leave…more people around me. Was too easy to lose control…alone. I felt I was living in a nightmare only I knew I would not be waking up, so ending it. The End…what would that be? Had there been An End already? Was Scott still alive? Ah, but we were at The Beginning…just barely…such a fragile beginning, I couldn't grasp its content; all I could think on was Scott's breathing…hanging on…being there when I arrived, but I was so afraid he wouldn't be…alive and breathing…hoping he would be; back and forth my hopes and fears warring with each other.

The first leg of the trip was into Atlanta…I managed. During the layover, I was afraid to call, afraid not to…my mind, such a mess. I mistakenly called my mother's number and heard her sleepy little old lady voice and realized what I had done, immediately hung up…then called my brother, Bud, and sister in law, Maxine…told them where I was and asked if they'd heard anything more…they hadn't.

Then, back into the air again…the closer I got, the more scared I became; couldn't talk, no one to talk to…finally I had to tell the nice man next to me what was waiting (?) for me in the St. Louis area…what had happened to my son. Talked to him all the way until the plane was landing. As soon as it stopped, I headed for the exit…a stewardess grabbed me and made me sit down, along with a stern lecture for leaving my seat before I was given permission to exit the plane. I explained to the mother and her young son sitting beside me…I later saw them at the baggage claim area, and she told me Scott was in her prayers…

When I got off the plane, Bud and Max and their daughter, Dena, were there waiting for me; also my Big Brother, Tuny. He'd flown in from Oklahoma to also be there when I arrived. I hadn't expected him to be…but was so very thankful that he was.

I finally got to that distant hospital; thankfully, Scott had survived the night. I don't remember clearly…it seemed a world of faces, but the only one I remembered distinctly afterward was Scott's girlfriend's, Rachel. She hugged me and told me she was glad I was there.

I had thought under the circumstances, Scott wouldn't want to see anyone, even me. He gave such courage by continued acceptance of visitors, family, friends. I said such dumb things when I got in to see him...so very glad to hear his voice, look into his eyes. I tried to make a joke about his new head gear: a two-tined metal fork with one prong over each side of his head, then screwed into the sides...wires with weights at the other end, attached to the "fork..." keeping his head/neck stretched tight, unable to move. I shouldn't have...realizing now all the questions in his mind as to what assortment of strange apparatuses were around him, attached to him, etc. But in spite of everything, he looked wonderful. I was there FOR HIM...but lovingly, even then, he was there FOR ME, too...a normally warm and welcoming "Hello, Mama..." It didn't matter so much, saying the right thing...I just didn't want to say the WRONG thing.

I had been up well past 32 hours before finally sleeping in the wee hours of July 1, in the small waiting room just outside Scott's hospital room. Scott's father slept on the other couch in the same room. There was still concern that Scott might have problems with swelling and would not survive the night.

I awoke around 5:30 a.m. and found my way to the cafeteria and the coffee pot. There was a small lake with benches and tables out beyond the patio area. I headed for the water with coffee in hand. As I sat there, thinking of what the past several hours had held...and that Scott was alive...I sensed, "God is in

His Heaven and all's right with the world." THAT felt so good…and then, I was taken aback by even having that in my mind with Scott laying up in that room, screws in his head, unable to feel anything, move his legs, arms…How could I feel all was right with the world…? But I realized the only thing that could put that into my head was God…and if He had said it to me, then I knew SOMEHOW it would be. He was there with us and held us as we went through the rest of it. He is still holding us near under His protective wings, I'm sure.

Roger found me by the lake. He heard me tell him how I'd never been a good "nurse…" my mother had always been good with that, but I wasn't. When Scott had a temporary tooth in place when he was about 12, I fed him corn on the cob and his tooth fell out. That's the kind of "nurse" I was. I hadn't been able to help Eileen with Lewis when he was sick, they were Jim's parents, Scott and Roger's grandparents; I just wasn't good at that kind of thing. He heard me tell him that I'd never wanted to remain alone before…but then, with Scott's situation before us, I was glad I was not even dating anyone. How could this be put on anyone else when I didn't even know how to deal with it myself; but on the other hand, I was free to be as Scott's needs required. That part was good.

There was another family sharing the waiting room with us. Scott had a companion in the Intensive Care Room who had undergone brain surgery and never recovered. Scott was aware of his roommate; and when he realized what was going on in that corner of the room, commented, "That's rough." With all he was going through, Scott was concerned for the other patient in ICU. His wife and I still correspond, usually at Christmas. We became a family, of sorts; the first of a series of remarkable people who would become dear to me through this tragedy we had just encountered.

When Scott and Roger were about 3 and 5, 4 and 6…we lived near friends who had sons the same ages, or nearly so. Both those family had suffered the loss of a son during the years in between our closeness and this newest tragedy. George and Shirley, Marty's parents, and Michael, Craig's brother, came to spend time either with Scott or with me. Our three families…our times all together had been precious times, but none of us could back up time and start all over.

Roger was with me when I talked with the doctor filling in for Dr. Krettek, Scott's surgeon, and was told Scott would ALWAYS NEED ME. He would always from this day on, be dependant on others for his care. He could not have painted a bleaker picture. Others were upset by that, but I wasn't. I believe in preparing for the worst case scenario, even with this. If you're ready for the worst, that most likely won't happen, so the rest is easier then. To me, Scott was alive…his death would have been "The Worst," so I was already on my way to acceptance before talking with the doctor. I just had to learn; but at that point, I really didn't even have a clue as to what there was to learn.

I had prayed and prayed that when the time came, I would have the right words…never would our clumsy words be more important; our only tools available for pulling Scott through to hope and what tomorrow would have in store. Roger had gotten to the hospital safely; Scott eventually asked to talk to just me and

Roger. It was so important to me to be able to help Scott KNOW he was so much more than that handsome, athletic, graceful hunk…but to simplify the efforts that would have to be made wouldn't have been honest either. Some words (?) that would encourage yet identify what lay ahead. He began with "I don't want to live this way…" Praying for the right words still while trying to speak the words…I began. I cannot remember exactly what was said except I started with how I'd always thought that if such an accident should happen to him or to Roger I hadn't thought I would want either of them to have to endure such a life, but I had discovered during the hours since Bud's call that wasn't how I felt at all, and that Mom had always told me he was a gift from God and not to love him too much because I might not always have His gift; how much it meant to find that the gift was still here to be loved when I finally got to him in the hospital. I then tried to emphasize the silent soul that made Scott the person we all loved; not the athlete or the young man with all the right "toys" and professional successes…the smile, the sharp and creative mind, the humor that was all still intact…all that really was Scott was still there. The rest had just been for show, for fun. Reality was the person inside that wasn't so obvious but was still a treasure. The hard part was learning how to live with, deal with this new life that was evidently ahead of him…There was no way to dress that up and make it sound like fun; just hopefully, beyond that he would find a whole new appreciation of the world around him. One that the rest of us just took for granted. Hopefully, he more than the rest of us, would really find the beauty and joy in the moment...eventually, but there was no denying that it would involve a lot of extremely hard lessons.

July 6, 1991.

MY GIFTS ARE CHERISHED

I would be more—Stronger—Fearless—
Yet not enough is shown.
He would be more—Patient—Fearless—
Yet horrors shout inside his wondering mind.
He is there and came alone
Through the dark of night,
Across miles of fearful travel.
We are together
And would be more
Until the needs are less.

My Gifts are cherished
But we are learning new words
And the process is confusing;
We are seeing, feeling new pain
And have yet to find some comfort.
We are lost with him in his present
And looking for the doors that open into
security.
We are each merely human
And desperately need God's strength and
guidance.

We are all afraid—together.

There have been very few mentions of death vs. the new reality since that original talk; but those discussions have occurred. There has also been the "allowance" for down times, times to say, "This sucks." Spinal cord injuries do not create "super men and women"; their basic stresses are enough, they don't need the added responsibility of making the rest of us "feel better" by acting like it's never hard and it never bothers them to be in a wheelchair, to be paralyzed, to not have their fingers to reach out hold something within their grasp, to feel softness or pain. We were finding a spinal cord injury to be everything you might think it would be, multiplied by 100, at the least!

In an instant, his life had changed. All of us, in any new circumstance or situation, need time to adjust. Such times can include a marriage, the birth of a child, a new home, a new job, even sometimes death when someone has been ill or is elderly and their time inevitably draws to an end…but in these events, we usually have time to start preparing, learning. We can try to be ready to deal with such changes in a timely manner. Not so with a spinal cord injury. In the blink of an eye…or a dive into the lake, or a traffic accident, or whatever…everything has changed forever.

One moment, there are trips to the bathroom to urinate or take a crapper…the next, there's a tube placed in your urethra and the urine is draining into a bag alongside the bed (other methods are eventually presented for choice); time in "the library" is replaced by a bowel program. If you're "lucky," in time you'll graduate to being placed onto a chair which sits over the commode and you'll be able to complete your bowel program with more dignity; this, only if you have an accessible bathroom. Catheters, suppositories (fondly called "silver bullets") and antibiotics to fight recurring urinary tract infections become part of daily life.

But these were not the considerations during those first "few" days. We were at the beginning place of learning and were so ignorant.

My little 81 year mama was there, asked me what she could do to help. I told her to just stay well; I had nothing left to worry about anyone other than Scott, and Bless her strength. She held up remarkably well. She's 87 as I write…Scott talks on the phone every Sunday morning with both of his grandmothers. Eileen, my mother-in-law was also there. She had been almost as much a part of my youth as my own mother had been. Jim and I had started dating when I was 15; we were married when I was barely 17. When Scott's accident happened, Eileen had already lost a son when he was 16 in a car accident; Jim's father, Lewis, had not been well for years before he died. When I hugged Eileen, all I could say was "It never stops, does it?"

And what then was our (Jim and me, and Peggy, the step-mother's) responsibility? I read so many things, books, brochures, anything I could get my hands on to learn…as I've already written, I read nothing about "transfers" and was devastated when the reality of Scott's future movements was presented before my eyes. Neither was there anything written by another parent. There was not one "other" I could identify with, ask, lean on. THAT is the reassurance I hope this writing presents; not a "how to, when to, if" book…but a relative to the circumstances of other parents who find their child, younger or older, in such a devastating and immediate change. This mother is no expert beyond loving her children, having unashamedly basked in their accomplishments throughout their lives and then finding a way to continue all that had been in a completely new and foreign environment that had come about in the blink of an eye. As soon as I sat down and tried to put the words on paper though, I realized why there had been nothing to read. Just as Robert had to recall harder times when he placed that telephone call to this stranger, it is hard for this parent to recall those hard times with her son. We nurture, protect and guide our children…as long as breath is in our bodies, that is the essence of parenting. When our children are beyond our ability to nurture, protect and guide, there seems so little substance in what we are truly able to give. Side by side with the sight of our children dealing with paralysis, we ache to "fix it" for them…and cannot. Side by side with our pride in their determinations and accomplishments…are the invisible boundaries on assistance now placed around our child's sense of dignity and independence…so, usually impossible to identify gracefully.

Our responsibility? Just to not give up. Give into beaten moments, discouraging times…despair…long enough to get it out of your system. Then, grab hold and start the day again…over and over again, as long as it is needed. What other choice is there? Robin once told me, "It will get better." I wondered then, how? but it does…give yourself time to learn, to adjust. It's all right not to know everything. Don't place all hope on tomorrow…help your injured loved one deal with the present. In some miraculous "tomorrow" a cure may be available, but don't waste all the "todays" that are HERE RIGHT NOW waiting for that tomorrow that may never come. Our injured loved one needs to know NOW that he/she is still loved as he is right now, even with such a traumatic, dramatic, drastic instant change in the person he had been just a few short minutes, hours, days, weeks, months ago. Our priority need? Patience, Patience, Patience. A paralyzed life cannot be hurried, everything takes longer…we get impatient waiting to get our foods checked by the clerk in the grocery store; that loved one in a wheelchair can no longer do anything as quickly as he once did, and he would be elated to stand in line at the grocery store or any other place. Slow yourselves down. That part is good for your blood pressure regardless; and in turn, puts less pressure on the one who can't get there, do, move as quickly.

Jim and I seemed to be communicating well, but then the next time we'd be together and have a conversation, it would be so different that I would end up wondering, "what about what we talked about yesterday—or a few hours ago?" I'd FEEL the mother part of the parent discussion; but then, bang…I wasn't a part of anything. This was OUR son; I'd hoped we could be PARENTS together…for this at least. In the course of things, we tried to discuss what would be best for Scott. As Jim had always been so involved with Scott, I believed him when he told me not to make any major changes in my life. He assured me he would always be there for Scott. At one point, Scott's step-mother, Peggy, and I had a long talk. She wanted me to know she would be there for Scott as though he were her own son. At the time, sincere and honest intentions...we all had those, and I wanted to believe her.

Scott, Roger and I determined to celebrate any victory, large or small, as it came our way. By the time I got there, I could already celebrate: Life. We soon realized in Scott's condition, even breath was a victory. Life could have meant dependence on a ventilator; his level of injury dangerously close to that circumstance. By the 3rd or 4th day, he was moving his arms...another celebration. One hopes more and more will keep returning...in Scott's case, he had improved to the level of injury as diagnosed: C5/6 Complete. We couldn't realize that fully...but with the passing of time, one knows. This is it.

Eventually, Scott was placed in a bed that rotated...one side to the other ever so slowly to keep the pressure off his body. The evening they were placing him into the rotating bed was the day I finally took some time off and went to my mother's to sleep in a real bed that night. I had realized that would be an upsetting event for me to attend but afterward, I wished I hadn't left. I had expected they would prepare him for the transfer better, reassure him. Perhaps they've had enough experience, they know the injured one's mind really can't accept all the attempts at explanations so early.

When I was little...visits to the dentist, later with a broken arm when I was six years old that had to be set...I've always felt if someone would have talked to me about what to expect beforehand, they wouldn't have been such frightening experiences. I had always tried to explain situations to my sons when they were young and learning about the more difficult things in life. This time, how could we explain? We knew so little ourselves...so far beyond anything we'd ever allowed ourselves to even think on.

The new rotating bed would be almost perpendicular in its fullest swing...which made it easier for those of us with Scott, trying to talk to him, but Scott's medicated mind plus his loss of sensation created a nightmare of events for him. He didn't know where he was; he thought he was going to fall; he had hallucinations...horrible ones, funny ones, tender ones. He couldn't sleep. I'd been to the chapel, just praying that Scott could have a few moments of real rest, sleep...and it happened, briefly. When he went to sleep, I sat down in the chair, instantly went to sleep myself...and I snored. When I snored, that scared Scott and woke him up; we were right back where we had started.

He had read a book, Weaveworld. He thought he was in the rug like the characters in the book and was afraid that if he went to sleep, he would die. I hated that book and wished it had never been written. In '95, I finally got that book and read it to find more about Scott's source of fear during that awful night in July '91. It's a greatly entertaining book written by Clive Barker; just a bad focus for hallucinations.

He couldn't know what he was in; he was afraid he'd fall. I tracked down a picture of the bed...took it into Scott, following the bed's path from one side to the other, tried to help him understand. I described everything, his body's placement, the cushions and straps…I showed him the picture. Nothing worked, and when the nurse, Rose Ann, came in I demanded that she stop the damned bed just for a few minutes. Of course, she couldn't do that and the next morning, I apologized to her. I so wanted to give Scott some brief relief…and couldn't find a way to do it. I tried to explain that he was in a bed that was protecting his skin and his lungs, rotating him so pressure would not build up at any given time on any area of his body. I told him where all the supports were placed, how it worked, that not a hair on his head was moving as the bed rotated…that not one tiny part of him was unstable or unsafe on that bed. He could not comprehend any of what I tried to tell him.

It is impossible to relate to what Scott's mind and senses were dealing with; the nerves still trying to relay messages that could no longer get through. To no longer have the ability to MOVE or to FEEL…How can a mind that is used to feeling the sock or the shoe on the foot, the weight of the sheet or blanket across the body, the soft skin being touched by the fingers…fathom what has happened when sensations no longer exist?

Neither pleasure nor pain have remained as physical indicators of well being or even of existence below mid-chest.

Another time, he thought he was in an opium den with knives in the ceiling and people were looking at us, listening to us…he wanted me to get him out of there and got angry at me because I was talking too loudly. I finally just asked him to please trust me, to know I was telling him the truth…that everything was okay, no one was there or listening to us. He got so angry at me, emphasized that he was telling the truth also…by this time which was around 6:30 in the morning after a LONG, HARD night, I had nothing left and had to leave the room, crying. Roger was asleep in the waiting room; I woke him up and asked him to go in and take over. Rachel was asleep on the other bed in Scott's room, but she needed to sleep just as we all did so I didn't waken her. I went to sleep and Roger helped get Scott through the rest of the night. Later when I went in, Scott apologized for having given me such a rough time…I told him he had nothing to apologize for—and he didn't—but those words were precious.

Once when I went up to him, he told me to watch out for the piano wires. Rachel asked him what wires, and he told her the ones over my head. He was trying to protect me…didn't want me to get hurt…Some hallucinations were innocent, and we played along. The ones that were frightening were very difficult to get through; reassurance was impossible.

Roger and I rode up together to see the rehabilitation center in Springfield, Illinois, that had been recommended. I was dead on my feet; we both looked ragged and tired; my mind was just sludge. I drank Gatorade; to this day, when I drink it, I remember that drive. We had to get oil put in the car, then forgot to put the bolt back on something…had to turn around and find it along the roadside. I couldn't talk; the words were right in my mind but when I'd hear myself talking, the words were all coming out wrong. I couldn't remember names…I finally started crying and told Roger I was going to stop talking, I was sounding like a retard. He told me it was all right, that I hadn't slept…that was all. It's wonderful to have sons who put you back together when you're falling apart. My sons were legal adults by the time we got into this situation; I was so blessed with the understanding, sensitive Men I found they had both become when I needed it most.

In Springfield, we'd never been to a spinal cord rehab center so had no comparison to make but found it to be clean and seemed well maintained. The staff used the word "quadriplegic" in describing Scott. I asked them to define it, as I was still stuck on the old definition and as Scott could move his arms, was breathing on his own, I hadn't been able to accept that word as relating to Scott. Their definition was something to the effect that all four limbs were affected…and even though Scott could move his arms, he didn't have use of his hands or fingers. I don't know what they saw on my face; I felt I was being a good listener, being educated and learning all I needed to know about Scott's situation…but inside, I felt I'd been cut by a knife. It was so easy for them to say "it" and so hard for me to hear it. We took photos of the place to take back to Scott so he could see it and "meet" the staff who would be working with him. When he got there, the "new" faces maybe wouldn't seem like strangers.

Paralyzed, Quadriplegic, and Broken Neck…the order in which I eased into these new terminologies. Before the accident, I would have thought these words and an ease in using them would have occurred in the reverse order…"Broken Neck" is still the most painful to me; perhaps because without knowledge of those two words, the rest would not have occurred. I would choose never to have learned what a broken neck can do to a person's life. Anything that is forced upon us so violently can never become a comforting companion in life.

Scott had to wear an oxygen mask that seemed to constantly be slipping up, climbing over his eyes. As quickly as we'd get it placed back into a comfortable position for him, it would start sliding up or down or over or around something. After DAYS of only intravenous nutrition and fluids, we were finally able to give Scott some ice water. We couldn't give him ice chips. I can't clearly recall why not; I'm sure something to do with the possibility of his choking but it may have also had something to do with the fact that when he broke his neck, some of the bone fragments also damaged his esophagus, so he was even more susceptible to choking. Anyway, it came about that we could fill a syringe with water and squirt it directly into Scott's mouth. Ice water: I'm sure nothing will ever taste BETTER to Scott. I can still see the brothers: Roger was in charge of fluid control; Scott was in charge of enjoyment.

The time came, I knew I would have to return to Orlando and work. I WOULD HAVE STAYED…That would have been my only choice; except especially now, I had to work…to get ready for…? There are no words to describe how I felt when I went in to tell Scott I was ready to go. There was a reality and truth in my head for what I knew I had to do, but I heard Scott saying how he would take care of things if I "wanted" to stay…WANTING TO STAY was all I wanted to do…but I couldn't. I left with his words in my ears and wondering if I was doing the right thing...I told him I would be back in 3 weeks. From the time he had been moved into the rotating bed and still when I had to leave, he was totally disoriented. He couldn't perceive where he was or what was around us. He continued to KNOW all of us, respond in rational ways for the most part which made it even harder for us to recognize the rest of it. He seemed mentally stable, but he wasn't. We were so intent on the tubes and moving bed and the damage to his spinal cord and what might lay ahead, we didn't realize what was happening inside his malfunctioning mental circuits.

Before I left St. Luke's, Peggy and I talked; she wanted to assure me she'd be there for Scott, as I had been. She meant it; but within 48 hours, she had called me in Orlando and said she had tried...but when he continued his hallucinations, she just couldn't deal with it; she didn't know how I had managed. She had tried; I appreciated that...I didn't know how I had managed either...except he was my son; how could I not?

I left the hospital after having spent time with all the doctors, nurses, counselors...with all their telephone numbers and their reassurances that I could call any time I wanted to (and I did). Unbelievably, sitting in the terminal at the airport on my way back to Orlando, I heard a familiar voice right next to me! It was a dear friend from Orlando, Lynn Cline, who had been in the area to visit her family. Nothing like that had ever happened before; nothing like that will most likely happen again. Lynn being on that flight with me, even though we weren't sitting near each other, kept me whole during the flight.

All the hours and days of that first horrific week…just ONE LONG UNENDING DAY…not broken into days and nights…just ALL ONE PIECE OF SUSPENDED, HURTFUL, FRIGHTENING TIME…

Roger stayed a few days more; he was there when they put the halo jacket on Scott. He also experienced Scott's "titty tomatoes" hallucinations along with Rachel which proved amusing, and the dreadful affects of sinus drainage on his brother, which was not. He saw the hospital they'd decided to take Scott to in St. Louis for rehab rather than the one in Springfield, Illinois. We'd both been pleased with what we had found in Springfield; he was rather close mouthed about what he had seen in the other. The first time I called Scott in his new surroundings, there was no answer in his room so I finally called the nurse's station. Whoever was on duty there, and I'm glad I never found out…told me, "Oh yes, he just walked back into his room." If insensitivity is grounds for termination of employment, that person would instantly have been without employment in those particular surroundings. If only it really was that way…I still get angry when I remember. When he first arrived and for several days afterward, he was placed in the last room down the hall, by himself. Quads cannot "yell" loudly; even their sneezes are almost unrecognizable as such. He could not press the call button. If he got in trouble, there was no way for him to get immediate help. It wasn't until I got there many days later that he was moved to a room just across from the nurse's station.

Starting at the acute care center and continuing at the rehab "center," Scott got hundreds and hundreds of cards. When I got there, I put them on strings along the top of the wall, like with Christmas cards. They almost circled his room, and this way he could look at them...see how many were thinking of him. They were taken down by the staff...the positive reinforcement had turned into a safety hazard. Of all the hazards Scott was facing at that time, those cards as a safety hazard was the least of them!

Scott wanted Rachel there; Rachel wanted to be there. Through the next several months, she made the difference in so many things for Scott. There can be no second-guessing or re-doing. I thank her for all she did; I'm glad she is getting on with her life and doing well. She was our angel; before I went back the first time, I searched the stores to find just the right statue of an angel to take back and give to her. I needed to remain involved enough that should circumstances and their relationship change, I would still comfortably KNOW what Scott was dealing with, how I could help, what not to expect or try to do so Scott could remain as secure as possible with this potential replacement. Trying to do that without interfering was my intent; understandably, it was not always well taken...and I was MOM, sometimes right or wrong, I felt it was my right and obligation. Basically, independent decisions, wise choices and deliberate actions had always been what I had strived to provide as a parent. Whether I was successful or not, these were values I wanted to encourage...and quadriplegia demanded that these life tools be used.

I understood Scott's need for Rachel's presence; I so appreciated her presence but feared for her ability to withstand the coming days and the dependent position she was putting herself in. Selfishly, I wanted anyone, anything there that could help Scott. The time would come for his "independence" again...but his mind needed this loving, beautiful young girl by his side, and I wanted that for him. She was there...reassuring him, loving him, talking to him; so supremely confident that tomorrow would be all right.

After Roger came back, we talked...we both questioned our "what to do's." I told Roger we just had to do what felt right in our hearts and to expect that we would make mistakes. We all had to accept that even the mistakes were made with love; there were bound to be a lot of those. We were all aliens in a foreign country; without knowledge of its customs and requirements. The words "made sense" but comprehension was shallow.

I came back after Hell Week and went to work on Monday morning; I felt I had been away, on a distant planet for months. I felt like I'd never driven a car before, it was a struggle to remember how to drive, where to go when I was on my way. At work, the phone, the computer, the files...others around me were carrying on in their usual way; I felt so lost...none of the realities seemed real anymore. Reality was laying in a hospital bed back in Missouri. The elevators going up and down just reinforced my sense of still being at the hospital with Scott. I had always gone out to my car over the lunch hour to read and just watch people. When I got back from Missouri, if my car was parked toward the street...sidewalks, a bus station, people walking, walking, walking…I couldn't bear to watch them. I would think 'you are so lucky and you don't even realize what a wonderful gift you have'. I would watch arms swinging, hands grasping a bottle or a can, legs bending at the knees, one foot going in front of the other. It must have been similar to what a person in jail or prison must feel when given glimpses of FREEDOM. Freedom vs. entrapment inside one's body, or trapped inside a building…loss of FREEDOM. I couldn't bear to watch people do what Scott couldn't do anymore. How could I do things Scott couldn't do? How could any of us be happy when paralysis exists…It is so awful. I was swallowed up by all the losses. It took time and more problems and mistakes to find out ALL was not really lost; Scott wasn't totally fragile and vulnerable but at that point, I was just in the "hang on" phase. I had no idea what I was hanging on TO…but just knew it would be even worse if I "let go."

God forever bless my dear friends who called and talked and helped keep my mind occupied 'til I could get back up to Scott, and all those who helped "fund" my flights back and forth during the next several months. I knew I had good neighbors, but Fred and Sharon's help was above and beyond what I could have expected; they became my lawn care staff all that summer. With all the calls and trips, there was not time to mow the grass. I don't know what I would have done without them. My friend, Kathy, and her husband Freddy whose twin brother had been injured several years back, a quadriplegic since…Kathy is no bigger than a minute, but has the heart and strength of a mythical giant. She shared so much with me of what they had learned; she ever so kindly taught and prepared me. I lost weight, back down to what I had been before Scott was born 28 years earlier. Work and the telephone, my constants…and with Ma Bell's assistance, I could call and talk to Scott, make sure he was all right…didn't feel quite so separated from what he was going through and that was the only way I could have dealt with the miles between us. The difficult part of that was if I called and there was no one in the room to pick up the phone, I knew Scott would be distressed having no way of answering the phone…so to only let it ring a few times? Or to let it ring forever until someone eventually answered? Recognizing that dilemma, we decided on a time it would be best for me to call so all could be in readiness there when I did (in the form of an assisting hand). A voice phone worked best for Scott, but then we were without private conversation. Eventually, it was set up that all he had to do was push a button…so could answer the phone without assistance. When there is an illness, an accident, a death in someone's family, never hesitate to get in touch.

You won't be interfering. Someone out there, listening, made me feel so much less alone and frightened. You have no idea how very important that support is…unless you've been there.

During my three weeks back in Orlando, I met Robin, met Michael and had several visits with him. I had ordered and received the Spinal Network spiral bound book for Scott, the A Guide to Spinal Injuries for Patients and Family for myself and had subscribed to Spinal Network magazine. I had read my book cover to cover, highlighting passages, making notes and had reviewed Scott's book on the first flight back to St. Louis. When I was there, I knew Scott was being mentally barraged with each hour's adaptation to the new territory his paralyzed body now inhabited in addition to the physical problems that went along with that and with the enormous emotional stress related to acceptance of same; I left the things I'd brought for Scott, Rachel and his father to read and research. We all had to come independently and in our own time to the places where we could absorb the words, instructions and suggestions for learning about quadriplegia. Note: It was December '92 before Scott opened his Spinal Network and began to read it. My Guide remains one of the most important books on my bookshelf.

Michael had been hit by a car…the car was stolen, the driver was wanted by the police. Scott had foolishly chosen to dive into what proved to be shallow water. Scott's injury was self-inflicted; Michael's had been placed on him by a stranger. A SPINAL CORD INJURY…the definition is "simple." The rest is not. Each injury has immediate differences that extend out, becoming more and more complex. This basic difference in the cause was my initial introduction to varying perceptions. At the time, we thought Scott had insurance; Michael did not…another variance which later proved untrue. Neither had insurance. I'm still not sure but think that lack was the reason the rehabilitation center in Springfield, Illinois was not chosen for Scott; I was not a part of the decision or discussion for whatever reason. When I found so many resources available in Orlando, even without the "luxury" of insurance, my hope grew that some way, someday Scott could travel those many miles to benefit from services offered here. During those times when just getting from the bed into his chair was a major journey, hope remained alive and constant.

Michael was so cold, so I took a green afghan to him; one that my mother had made. I had made a mauve colored one earlier for Scott, so asked Rachel to take it down to the hospital, so he'd have it nearby if he got cold…and he did during my next trip up…shivering, teeth chattering just like Michael. I had spent so many hours working on that afghan for him, making sure it was l-o-n-g enough to cover my tall son…and there was love in every stitch, but the extra work and extra stitches so extra love couldn't wrap Scott tight enough to keep him warm.

CHAPTER TWO

…And Rehabilitation Follows

So I returned…four weeks approximately into the injury. ELEVATORS, ELEVATORS, ELEVATORS at St. Luke's, at my work, at the rehab center, at Humana back in Orlando. I don't think I'll ever enter one without feeling I'm on my way to Scott's room at one of the hospitals we were becoming too well acquainted with. For so long, our lives were hospitals and elevators. A hospital became my second home over the months as they passed slowly by. My first return to St. Louis (end of July/first of August, 1991)…Day One: Scott was transferred.

It was the first time I saw Scott in the halo jacket. The original screws and headgear were replaced by new screws and lightweight rods (two behind and two in front) which were attached to a jacket lined with fleece. The broken bones in his neck were replaced with a custom made plate; the halo jacket was to insure that his neck was kept absolutely immobile while the plate surgery and placement healed. When I first walked into his room, he was up in his chair…complete with halo jacket and a smile on his handsome face. He had a muscle tee-shirt on (no sleeves) and the loss of bulk in his shoulder and neck area affected me more than the halo, but I couldn't react. In three short weeks, he had lost so much; as though it had melted away…like an ice cube tray full

33

of frozen cubes sitting in the sun. The substance was still there, but the form had changed so much.

It is so hard to remember everything and at the time, I couldn't record it. My mind was too full; there were too many questions. It was a nightmare that I didn't want to remember later; all I could do was get through this day, this hour, this minute. There was no way to put it on paper at the time. I tried sometimes; only a few words would be written...and in no order, only fragments of a thought, or a fear...

This time, Scott was at the new facility...for "rehabilitation" (vocational and physical). I was able to stay in a room just across the street, actually a part of the hospital at a very reduced rate. This way, I was able to be with him all day and experience the whole routine of his day. I just wanted to know HOW so many things; in case...I never cathed him; but I watched how it was done. I shaved him once and found out it's much easier to shave my legs than my son's face! I didn't want my invasive hands intruding on him unless it was needed; I was torn between needing to know how and respecting his dignity and privacy. Always trying to find the balance...in this and so many other intimacies. Even pushing his chair into therapy, a trivial challenge, seemed difficult...the locks to be placed in gear or disengaged, pieces to be removed and replaced if he was going to be transferred...a chair with wheels had become a puzzle with endless pieces to be placed absolutely perfectly! I would go to my room shortly after Rachel's return in the evening, allowing them private time together for the rest of the evening.

Rachel and I took Scott (all wrapped up in blankets because he was so cold) through the tunnel under the street over to the building where I was staying…our first "adventure." Scott was already shivering because he was so cold; I had told them but don't think they believed me…the rooms where we "visitors" were staying, were like one big freezer! Taking him on the "tour" proved interesting but brief…they couldn't deal with it (I wonder how I did…but was so thankful there was a convenient room at a cheap price; that part far out-weighed the polar-like climate control!). We got back down (in the elevator) to the lobby and checked to see if there was another way to get Scott out of the building and back to the other place other than using the tunnel again. There was a side door with a ramp, so we went out that way…then, trying to get across a busy street…Scott wrapped up, halo-ed, wheelchaired…had to be one of the funniest or most warped moments of my life! This was to prove a constant in Scott's struggle…he never hesitated to DO! He never doubted he COULD.

One evening, Jim was coming by after work. Scott, Rachel and I waited outside, curbside, to watch for him. Peggy and Eileen came that evening also. Scott watched the cars going by with the enthusiasm of a novice, old pro car trader that he was! He hadn't been OUT…to watch, see traffic before that evening since his accident. So many "firsts" ahead of him in his "new life": outings with the group from rehab, out in a car, at home overnight, for a week-end…I was so proud of Scott for each determined effort; so frightened for him at the same time.

I was totally unprepared for the transfers. My mind was so saturated with thoughts of Scott's inner personal "well being"; that kind of thing just hadn't crossed my mind. I had never seen or thought of a "transfer." When I was a child, I had grown up with a dear family friend from our little country church in Illinois, Mt. Nebo Primitive Baptist Church, who had multiple sclerosis. To me, Marion was Marion. His father would carry him into church on his back holding his arms around his neck, and place him in his chair by the window. Now, I think of those times as "transfers." Just as new friends accept Scott as he is today; that's how I knew Marion. There were no other times and ways of living. I didn't recognize the pain his family lived with; I comfortably and innocently loved and enjoyed my friend, Marion. Our times together, playing board games…maybe helped prepare me for what was to come so many years later.

I suppose I thought in this day and modern age of technology, surely everything was streamlined and "easy" and there had been nothing written in my book for Patient and Family about transfers. One has to be able to move about; not hard one thinks! My first exposure was made harder by the method used; Scott and Rachel both told me later that had been that particular therapist's first session with him and that had been the first time he had been transferred in that manner. At the time, my mind was thinking this was how it would always be and the full measure of the non-control my son had over his body was forced visually upon me. (Scott is 6'5" of handsome young man; transfers would be much easier if there weren't so much of him to be transferred!) The therapist had him bent double, with his face looking down at his feet; no dignity remained for my son. My heart was breaking inside but on the outside, if this was the way it had to be…then, Scott could not realize how it was affecting me. I would have to accept it and get beyond it.

One evening, Scott wanted us to put him into bed; I assumed Rachel knew how to do it and taking a deep breath of determination, we attempted the transfer. If my brother, Bud, had not walked in exactly when he did, I am sure Scott would have ended up on the floor; and if the nursing staff had known what we were doing, we would probably have been forbidden to ever visit Scott again! This added nothing to my "confidence" in my ability to do a transfer although it "helped" to realize afterward that Rachel had never done a transfer either. And, my brother was grand…not a situation he would have volunteered to handle I'm sure, but when duty called…he stepped in and "fixed."

Fortunately, there are more graceful means and methods of transfers than the first one I saw which I later thankfully realized. When I got back home to Orlando after this visit, Roger and I practiced on each other. Scott was transferred by others with his head over their shoulder; some used a slide board from the bed to the chair, or to the mat, or back to the bed. Even those though being done by attendants with more expertise finally pulled out all my strength and ability to bear. I "held up" until they had to transfer Scott back and forth repeatedly trying to get him into a "new" chair; one that would be more comfortable for a 6'5" quadriplegic. I had reached my limit for coping with what he was enduring and had to leave the room. Fortunately, Rachel came in just as I was leaving so I was hoping my absence wouldn't be noticeable. I had to go outside and be a Mom. My fears and hurts and stresses overflowed in tears. Eddie Townsend was the attendant who most gracefully transferred Scott; he came out to check on me and talk with me, helped me get through the moment. Later, he helped me learn how to do transfers. He was with us when I overcame my fears and did it!

There is equipment designed for transfers from the bed, to the chair...we've not had that luxury so far (June '97); perhaps one day. The expenses...medical, equipment, etc. continue one way or another; yet the financial security is perhaps ahead; we haven't found that yet. ADA strives to improve accessibility while cuts in Medicare threaten the means of having adequate attendant care...and on and on...Scott is one of the more fortunate ones; some are more so...others less...but the help that should be readily available (economically beneficial for everyone) is provided in a less than secure manner; the decisions and procedures and processes are in the bureaucratic hands of those who have never even sat in a wheelchair, who can't imagine what it is like not to be able to use their fingers much less walk across the room, who look at the dollar signs as opposed to human lives and potential productivity. Often, those who could educate and speak most effectively are understandably intimidated by the powers that be. They must suffer inadequate services rather than rock the boat...possibly offend the powers providing their most basic, supremely important care; possibly end up with less than they have somehow managed to obtain. Their dignity and pride are their most important assets aside from their determination to get on with an independent life. These assets are not easily recognized by those providing services when schedules are tight, qualified personnel unavailable, staffs short, personal contact impossible, and inadequate funds impossible to be allocated fairly.

As with my home, I couldn't live somewhere Scott couldn't get into…and I live in a mobile home; not usually real accessible. I had a ramp built on. At the time, Scott was 1,000 miles away and with present circumstances, it seemed impossible that he could ever get down here again; but I prepared for that, and it eventually happened. Likewise, I had to KNOW I could transfer Scott. I wanted him to realize and know that I could.

He was so fragile then, but we could only know that when October and November rolled around and there was such a difference. We had learned so much by then…but still, the lessons continued.

Feeding Scott sounds relatively simple once you get beyond the hurt from the knowledge that your grown son can't feed himself any longer…but it wasn't. The broken bones in his neck had damaged his esophagus, so there were moments of terror even in something as simple as a bowl of beef stew. One of my most terrifying personal moments is when I choke, get strangled on something…so something I could totally identify with when it happened to Scott while I was feeding him. His eyes went up in his head, he passed out. I was screaming for a nurse, some help, anybody. God Bless Debbie…I had misjudged her before. She seemed the least involved and caring of the staff until her instant response and concern when that happened. My bones had turned to mush as soon as the crisis was over, and I had to sit down. Scott asked me to do something; I had to tell him I couldn't move until I had bones to support me again.

During this trip, I saw the war of temperatures as I'd seen with Michael...so extremely cold, teeth chattering; but if blankets were piled on, his temperature would go up too high. The loss of the ability for the body to regulate temperature, a broken thermostat accompanies the broken neck. Sweat has now replaced "pain" as a warning, not a bodily process used for cooling the body. We became better acquainted with dysreflexia and also muscle spasms.

I saw a rise in blood pressure bring about fainting spells. A binder around Scott's chest and abdomen helped maintain that. His chair would have to be tipped back, allowing his blood pressure to regulate itself. There was a lot of talk about pressure sores and Scott's learning to do weight shifts (pressure releases) when in his chair, but I hardly saw it practiced. There was a "spot" on his butt...a lot of attention given to it, but no action was prescribed. There were range of motion procedures to be learned and practiced and new equipment, like splints for his hands and his feet at night.

I talked with Scott's doctor, Mary Mukes, about not being there every day, about leaving. I asked her how many mothers had to leave like that, couldn't stay. I'm glad I asked that because she told me I would be amazed at how many mothers come once and never return. I asked her how they could not; she couldn't answer that but her first answer had been reassuring. She had made me feel better about leaving. The long week went by...it was time to come back to Orlando again. This time, I had a whole new list of names and phone numbers.

With the choking episode so vivid in my mind, during the time away I was most afraid of it happening again. Was so afraid that wouldn't improve...but thankfully, it did; and in time, Scott was feeding himself again. Last month (March '97), he told me it's not easy to eat an Egg McMuffin. I had taken breakfast when I went to visit him. I asked him when he'd had his last one...it was before his injury! We both enjoyed those Egg McMuffins...the challenge and the success adding nutrients to his increasing life skills, few as simple as conquering an Egg McMuffin.

Back in Orlando, I got Roger's book of names/addresses...sent out at least 50 letters...I'd say 75% of those who didn't respond was because their addresses were no longer correct. I got so many back for that reason. I wanted something special to add surprises and smiles to his days, little mini-vacations for his mind to travel to. Big Bird was the first to let Scott know he was thinking of him...he sent Scott a tail feather in a letter! Tim Conway, Lou Ferrigno, Loni Anderson, Whitey Herzog of the St. Louis Cardinals and William Devane sent autographed photos. Scott was most pleased to get a photo and letter from John Travolta. He was so excited when that arrived. Besides writing to Scott, both John Travolta and Walter Cronkite wrote me as well. That they would take time to write Scott was beyond gratitude from this mother's heart; that they would go even further and write to me emphasized the goodness and the sincerity of these two men who do honor to the public lives they lead. They are our heroes.

Since the time of that writing, John Travolta has become a father and has newly-blossomed in the field of "stardom"; he richly deserves all the successes already come and those yet to be.

(September, 1997. Princess Diana's tragic death. John Travolta was interviewed, and he said he wanted the young Princes to know he was available to help, that he'd been through tragedies and knew he could BE THERE for them, could help. I watched and listened and said to myself and to the TV screen, "Yes, you have been John Travolta, and yes, you can/do help." I wish he could have heard me.)

I wrote to the Orlando Magic and asked for the team to send something to Michael who was still going through rehab in Orlando. They sent him an autographed photo of the team, and a poster of Stuff the Magic Dragon. I hope he eventually was able to pass them along to his son, Miguel.

I had gone to a Family/Patient support group meeting at Humana Lucerne's Spinal Rehabilitation Center here in Orlando (no longer existent unfortunately). I had gone to the more private support group meeting, for those in chairs. They accepted my presence although I was able bodied and my son was 1,000 miles away. Both groups fed me with hope that I could take back to St. Louis with me on my next trip up. I finally met Robert; also John, Al, Ricardo and so many others...and eventually, John's mother, Gay. I found out about Normandy Manor, the Center for

Independent Living (also, no longer existent although other facilities in another location was found).

My next trip to St. Louis, there were no surprises...such as "transfers," and I was better prepared; I was better educated and I had HOPE to share.

Scott had written his name and saved it for me. I still have that first new "autograph." Not being able to write his name again, I had used one of his old letters to me and had a name stamp made. I don't think he ever used it; but he still had his "signature" if needed.

There were some adjustments needed for his halo jacket; so I was there when they transferred him onto the mat and loosened the jacket. It was the first (and probably the last) time he was on his stomach since his accident. Unfortunately, none of us realized his muscle t-shirt had slipped under the jacket. The whole thing had to be redone later when it was discovered to be so. I had an awful dream from that after I got back to Florida, felt so guilty for not realizing the shirt was there...and of course, Scott couldn't feel that it was there...it could have damaged his skin.

I dreamed I was in this big place, like an institution...or auditorium, with lots of halls and rooms and doors. I found Scott's wheelchair but couldn't find him. I was looking wildly through all the rooms, trying to find him...there was an "evil" man in one room, he followed me into another one. I told him to leave me alone, but he came after me and started to grab me. I grabbed a chair and hit him over and over and over with it, literally beating him to pieces. I'd never felt such utter hate and contempt for another living person. Then, I looked around and Roger came in except he was 3 or 4 years old, little, still at that fat, cute and giggly age…and he had Scott's muscle tee-shirt on, the one that had been left under the jacket. It was hanging off his shoulders, bunched up on the floor around his feet. He was so short, and the shirt was so long. I felt so bad looking at him but he was so proud to have Scott's shirt on…then, there were hundreds of us outside, looking for Scott. Up and down, over and around hills…green and grassy, flowers, fresh air…like at the sidewalks and grass at Disney World (I kind of felt like I was going over the bridge to the Haunted Mansion)…and that's when I woke up. I've always felt that evil man I beat into pieces was "quadriplegia…" having found a way to kill it in my dream at least gave some release; or perhaps I was killing my fear of it. Learning how to live with its presence in our lives didn't seem so insurmountable any longer. That dream had been so full of frustrations, fears, angers, hate, hopes, losses, and fantasies.

I came to realize Roger's hesitation in commenting about the chosen rehab hospital. When Scott was admitted, there was one other young quad there, who was released shortly thereafter. Otherwise, this was a center for rehabilitation of stroke victims…naturally, most quite aged. Scott was not among a peer group; and although rehabilitation is required in both instances, the paralysis of a young man's body who has held strongly to complete mental faculties is not in any way comparable to an older person with both physical and mental faculties affected. A huge need for positive reinforcement had no comparable presence. There were no "others" to identify with;

there were no "others" to further educate the therapists and attendants, their expertise was in dealing with stroke victims, not quadriplegics. NO ONE SHOULD PROVIDE CARE AND/OR REHABILITATION TO SPINAL CORD PATIENTS UNLESS THEY ARE EXPERT IN THAT DEFINITIVE FIELD. Approximately 7 wasted months later plus the initial 3 months, Scott was able to experience the difference between the spinal cord injury experts and those who treat stroke victims. Unlike my and Roger's first trip to the rehab center in Springfield, Illinois, in the months that followed we had become better acquainted with quality service and could make comparisons and identify what was good vs. what was not.

Their situation is so far beyond the norm; their paralysis affects their whole system to the point that regular medical routines just are not applicable…from diagnosis to treatment. Experts should be an absolute requirement, but we must "make do." Quadriplegics are not a routine part of any general practitioner's day, and excessive medical costs do not allow for experts routinely.

During this visit, Scott told me later he'd seen pity in my eyes and couldn't deal with that. There may have been some…of course, it was a horrible situation for my son to be dealing with…but once, while in therapy and I was looking around at all the pitiful stroke victims, I was so relieved that he was the only "healthy one" in the room. There was a little old man who had briefly been in the room with Scott. In therapy, as they were trying to get him from the chair to the mat, his trousers fell down around his feet. The poor therapist didn't know which to do first; the little old man was looking so pitiful and of course "nakedly vulnerable." I walked over and told the therapist it was all right, I knew him and pulled his pants back up for him and fastened them so they wouldn't fall down again. These times in rehab were such personally intimate experiences; strangers sharing all levels of emotional and physical exposures of one kind or another…a naked body was only that, something to be covered or administered to. There were ambivalent feelings because my son wasn't as he had been and probably never would be…but he was relatively "healthy" in comparison. I even came home afterward and wrote a poem about it, one of the few times I could really WRITE about my feelings and what was happening.

August 14, 1991.

ONLY FEAR, NOT PITY

You're wrong, Dear Son…
You have misread the mirror of this soul;
You were so strong among the weakened spirits
And I rejoiced to sense the difference there.

Our cares…for each other…Exchanged.

You hurt for me because you think
I hurt for you because
I think you hurt for me
Is only part of this exchange.
We are…mother & son/son & mother…
Parts of each other.

If this exchange is so painful,
How much greater would be the pain for both of us
…Without the other part?
I accept and am grateful for the sharing;
I hope you can simply accept our bond.

Still, it is what is within the injured person…and so many elements beyond their self (i.e., support, financial and personal) that determines what will happen after rehab, however beneficial or otherwise the facility may be. When Scott got out of rehab, he went "home"; when Michael got out of rehab, he was sent out of town to a nursing home.

While in rehab, Scott was allowed to attend his high school class reunion. A few weeks earlier, I had doubted Scott would want to see anyone in his new situation. I was so proud of his strength; I was so afraid of his "exposure." It went "well." Scott had been a star athlete; he found support, discomfort, ignorance, acceptance, disappointment and comfortable acceptance. When he left rehab, he had already experienced what reactions might be awaiting him by old friends. I told Scott it would often be up to him to make others comfortable with the changes…and I always encouraged those who were concerned but "fearful," to go see Scott…spend time with him. I told them they'd feel better having done so; that was and is always true.

With the reunion coming up, Jim returned one evening to practice getting Scott into a vehicle…brought one of his trucks down, thinking that would be easier. Eddie was there to help. He, Jim and Rachel worked on trying to get Scott into the truck…it didn't work. Peggy and I were both there. I tried to remain calm, stayed at the edge of the activity; close enough to see how things were going; far enough away that if I gasped or made a startled sound, they wouldn't hear me. They tried it again another evening. That time, it worked. Jim turned around with blood streaming down the side of his head where the halo had "grabbed him."

Scott's first trip back to Greenville, Illinois (about 50 miles east of St. Louis), was in a Chrysler LeBaron convertible; the only thing they could easily get him into with halo and all. I had read Joni's book...and remembered how she'd fallen forward in a vehicle because the driver didn't realize that she couldn't hold herself back, like when the brakes are stepped on, or for a sudden stop...but then, she hadn't been braced in a halo at the time either. Rachel was the driver, and they were going to Scott's father's place. I was a nervous but trying-to-be-confident mother waiting at my own mother's in Greenville; and when I hadn't heard from them yet, I called to see if anything had been heard yet from the "kids..." was asked "Why do you ask?" My "perception" of Scott's injury and his father's "perception" of Scott's injury might as well be two entirely different injuries. The "Why do you ask?" coming from Peggy, Scott's step-mother, might very well have meant, "Why? Is something wrong?," but I heard it as "Why do you ask, there's nothing to worry about." To me, there was everything to worry about, and I did not react kindly to the question. Just like the attendant who said Scott had just walked back into his room, I was extremely sensitive to the words used.

She later told Scott and Rachel I had been a bitch. Yes, I had been...

If I remember correctly, Scott had the day trip to Greenville...just mentioned, then later his first overnight trip which was also to Greenville. I had asked Rachel if she was comfortable with the responsibility...of the transfers in/out of the car, the caths, the problem area on his butt, his having to be turned throughout the night. She told me she wasn't, so I encouraged her not to just accept the requests of others but to speak up when too much was being expected of her. I told her I would support her feelings, but I couldn't speak for her. The time came...Scott, Jim, Rachel and I were in the room together. To start it off, I asked, "Rachel, are you wanting to do this?" I had given her her opening; she shrugged her shoulders and sweetly consented. This was typical of the place I'd find myself in. I couldn't tell Scott, Rachel doesn't want to do this or Rachel would have said it wasn't true. I couldn't speak for Rachel or it would seem I was taking over! I wanted to protect...both of them; to help any way I could to make it easier...support, trust, encourage or discourage, whichever seemed necessary at the time.

The importance of words is part of my nature normally and these were uniquely sensitive times. Words are all we have to communicate and usually prove clumsy tools in the best of circumstances. Some of us were learning a new language of words and feelings or lack thereof; some of us were just going on as though everything was the same. One would hope a centerline would be reached, but it didn't quite happen.

Rachel and I were with Scott when he went on his first "outing" with the rehab group. We were in a separate vehicle; Scott was on the van from the hospital with the other stroke victims in their wheelchairs. Scott had always been so proud of his height, but now his height was adding to the problems of paralysis. The halo added 2 or 3 inches to his "seated" height, getting into the van to go on the outings was not just a matter of being rolled onto the lift then, easily rolled back into the van. He had to be tipped slightly to get inside. We went to a mall and to a movie. Scott was in a manual chair and unable to push himself at this point. The halo received much attention, especially from children…adults were trying to be polite and not to look. The shops, the restaurants, the movie, the elevator in the mall…this time, viewed with accessibility in mind.

Recently (March, 1997), our President has experienced life in a wheelchair, albeit temporarily. I immediately thought, "Good…he will learn more fully how important accessibility is…" How can he not? It remains to be seen what will come from those lessons. His position and his personal experience can combine to make real contributions to improvements in accessibility problems for those in wheelchairs. With the extended realization that for some, it is not a temporary circumstance…permanent improvements can truly be made. May it prove to be so.

Relatively near the hospital, there was a row of sidewalk cafes. We would take Scott there to eat. Once my brother, Bud, joined us and pushed Scott's chair. Rachel and I were so careful when pushing Scott over the cracks and bumps; Bud had Scott in the

"Express Lane" comparatively. There were so few things to laugh about then…this one of those more humorous moments.

The skin doctor had looked at the small spot on Scott's butt. There was attention given to it but nothing was done beyond the observations. It wasn't felt it was a breakdown of tissue.

At some point, while I was in Orlando…between visits to St. Louis, Scott was experiencing chest pains. I finally called and talked with his doctor. Spasms…which we were learning about also. It felt to Scott like his lungs were jumping around inside him. What was really happening was the muscles in the chest area were spasming; it felt to Scott like the lungs were doing wild, frightening things…but in fact, it was the muscles around the lungs. Still frightening, but the explanation of what was really happening helped calm his fears.

Discussions were held relating to what next…after rehab. I felt accessible transportation was the priority; others didn't. I felt Scott should not make any permanent arrangements as far as housing until we all more fully realized what we were into; others didn't. Scott was not in a position to make his own choices or argue with those that were made. So, there was not accessible transportation available; instead, for MONTHS after rehab Scott was transferred in and out of a Mustang (mostly by Rachel) when he wanted to go somewhere…and would then usually stay in the car to visit someone. A "custom built" mobile home was purchased…supposedly to have all the accessible features including a shower Scott could roll into and out of (his only real specific request). The "accessible mobile home" was to be placed on his father's property in the country. I did not see the site nor the mobile home or plans for same until I went to visit Scott the end of October, 1991. I found then that more attention had been given to the selection of wall coverings and wood for the cabinets than the accessibility part.

I went to St. Louis this time "psyched"; it was TIME for me to KNOW I could transfer Scott. Really, I wasn't that SURE I could/would...but I was doing a mental battle in my mind; I can and will vs. I can't so I'd better not try. I didn't discuss this with anyone; this was my own tormentor. Actually, I told Scott I wasn't going to...I didn't want anyone else's expectations to exceed my own, and I wasn't sure; BUT one morning, before Scott was awake, (I think it was probably the day before I was to leave; so I knew it was "now or never") I asked Eddie to go into the waiting room across the hall from Scott with me. I told him I wanted him to show me HOW to transfer Scott and to let me practice ON HIM! This is such an intimately close situation. When our children are little, it's easy and natural to hold them close, to protect their head, arms, legs...it's another thing to have a 6'5" son so dependent upon you. It was easy to hold a little bundle of love; another thing to hold and support a larger bundle, weighing 150+ pounds and towering above your head. It had been hard even being that close to Roger while we "practiced"; it was even harder to get that close to a relative stranger, Eddie...but he had the expertise, the understanding, the sensitivity that would allow me to trust his closeness.

So...when Scott was awake, the bathing, dressing, cathing processes took place to the point he was ready to be transferred into his chair…and that's when I stepped in. I hadn't told Scott I was going to do it, and he said nothing as we defeated my fears! Eddie was on the other side, and I know helped…but I DID IT! I KNEW after that, IF IT EVER BECAME NECESSARY…I could take care of my son. I COULD TRANSFER HIM. Out in the hall, on our way down to therapy, he commented…"Mom, I thought you'd decided not to do a transfer…" I laughed and told him I hadn't been able to talk about it…hadn't been sure I would, but the time had come…I just HAD TO do it, and thanked him for his trusting cooperation and acceptance. Only later, did I realize I'd scraped my leg on the chair and something else, few small bruises. Nothing had hurt when it happened, I was only concerned about getting Scott safely into his chair. When I commented later to Roger about that, he told me I'd had so much Adrenalin flowing, I was feeling no pain! Probably true…I can almost understand those people who lift cars or tremendous weights to save something precious that is laying underneath. The mind…a huge resource, mostly untapped during normal circumstances.

By this time, late August, 1991…Rachel's stresses were more evident. Some of the staff at the facility had been talking to her about leaving Scott…I resented her talking with the staff about these things, but mostly…I resented her telling Scott what they were telling her. I felt she should have accepted their advice and left…or told them to keep their noses out of her and Scott's business…that it was up to her and Scott to decide what they had to do, either together…or separately, especially since she was so easily upset by comments I made. She would never tell me directly what I'd done or said to upset her; she'd just walk off and would later tell Scott what I had done wrong. Scott choked a second time while both Rachel and I were there with him…she just took her good, sweet time to respond as though it was no big deal. Afterward, Scott commented on her lack of concern. She told him if he didn't like the way she did things, to get himself another girlfriend and walked out the door. I tried telling Scott she was just scared; and as she was there so constantly, she was better off if she didn't feel the constant pressure, the need to be ready to react so quickly. I told him she'd burn out if she didn't give herself some space. I assured him everything would be all right; it had been a tense moment for everyone…to let it go. He was all right; that's all that mattered.

This would be my last trip up for a while. Scott would be released from rehab before his birthday (9/23); he would be busy adjusting to life after rehab. He and Rachel would be living with his father and step-mother until his mobile home was delivered and set up. We decided my next trip up would be in October. Settling in time was what Scott was needing. We would remain in touch often, but the setting and the needs were different. I went back to Orlando to wait…on stand-by if needed. Roger and Beth would go up in September for Scott's birthday…and for their father's which was three days after Scott's. That was his father's 50th and a major celebration and party was being planned for that event.

CHAPTER THREE

Home…and New Perceptions Therein

On September 14, 1991, Michael was discharged from Humana and went to a nursing home in Deland, about an hour from Orlando, Florida. It was an awful place; made worse by the fact that he had so few visitors from "home." The first time I went to see him (my friend, Louise, went along with me as I wasn't sure where I was going or how to get there), I found him sitting alone in his room, without his collar on. His head was hanging down, on his chest…tears were rolling down his cheeks. I hugged him, then asked him if he wanted me to put his collar on. He did. Eventually, when I realized he was not even being gotten out of bed on a daily basis; I asked that he be placed in his chair so we could go out on the patio during one visit and was told that no one there could get him into his chair. Now transferring Michael should not have been a huge difficulty; but most importantly, he should never have been in a situation where "no one on site could transfer him into his chair." At one point, I requested an audit of those facilities by the State, and an inspection occurred. Circumstances improved, but it was never a healthy environment for Michael. Unlike Scott's discharge from rehab in St. Louis, Michael was stuck out on a limb with no one around to care what happened or make enough noise to make sure he got attention and assistance.

Scott went to his father's home in Greenville with Rachel. They were going to stay there until delivery and set up of his new "customized" mobile home. In the meantime, there was "the party" to look forward to.

Life went on around us. Scott's accident hadn't affected the world...only his...only so many others around him. We all continued to live...in our own differing ways. Unpleasant events happened as well as pleasant ones, just like "real life" before paralysis. Any unpleasant ones written here serve only as this is what happened to us; how we/I dealt with this or that...not as a defense of my own actions, nor an attack on others. Perhaps you'll judge yourself less harshly if you relate to our less than perfect attempts at nurturing. Love, caring, concern is not always bestowed, translated, expressed in mutually understandable terms. We've all served our purposes...and in 1997, Scott is doing well; the end result smoothes over the bumps which sometimes appeared as inaccessible mountains on this new adventure on wheels...

Of course, Jim was entitled to a big "to do" and fuss over his #50...was good that happy times were being planned; he deserved those. Invitations were sent far and wide. In my mind though, there were two celebrations going on...and one wasn't even mentioned. Roger and Beth went; I stayed in Orlando and tried to figure out what to send Scott on this particular birthday; we'd never experienced one quite this way. Scott had always said he liked the shirts I got him, but shirts weren't even an "easy" gift this time...clothes take on a whole new practicality when they're being bought for someone who can't dress himself. Some "work," some don't, and we hadn't practiced shopping for the new Scott yet. I decided to send him an orchid, a white one. I'd never thought of that for anyone before, so decided it was almost special enough. It arrived in Illinois with a bloom on it, but hasn't bloomed since. I have it now, in Florida…it looks happy and healthy, just no blossoms! Later, Roger gave me photos…there was Scott with Roger and Beth and Rachel, sitting on the deck at his dad's, in his halo. By the time I got the photos, the halo had been removed. THEN, I was glad I had the picture…while he was in it, I hadn't thought I'd ever want a picture of him with it on.

That piece of metal screwed into his head held Scott so rigid and straight. In a way, he seemed more vulnerable after it was taken off…for a while. It got in the way during transfers and left its mark on those of us who did, but it also held him straight so he had more "protection." I felt he was bare and exposed when it was removed until we found, he was still all right without it…except his head leaned forward in the direction it had been slanted in for so many weeks. When Scott would see his reflection, he would say it looked like he was leaning forward, in a hurry to get somewhere, and he was right; that is what he looked like but no comments or suggestions or therapies were suggested that would indicate he didn't have to be leaning forward like that…so we all just accepted that's how it had to be.

The very worst conversation Peggy and I ever had or probably will ever have happened when Scott's new home was delivered. I knew Scott wanted the shower that he could roll into above all else. I asked Peggy if that had been worked out, and she told me no, but that wouldn't matter…it had a regular tub with a shower in it, and that would work out all right. I thought I had misunderstood her, so asked her again. She said Scott would just lift his legs over into the tub…blah, blah, blah…She went on to tell me she and Jim had already told Scott they would accept nothing short of his walking again…and that was when I realized I was talking to someone who thought she was God. Scott might walk again someday, but it would never be because his father and step-mother had told him he had to! If only it could have been that simple; if only they could have had that much power! I told her I thought we'd best change the subject as I was getting angry. She insisted upon continuing the conversation in the same vein and emphasized that she realized how I felt…at that point, I told her, No you don't. I have to go now. Good-bye.

As I wrote before, Scott's father and his stepmother and I perceived Scott's new circumstances from opposite sides of the reality. Later, with others…strangers…who were in the midst of Hell Week and Rehab that followed…there were all kinds of coping mechanisms in place emotionally. My priority was the reality of the moment always; that one we love NEEDS to know…this may get better; it may not. Regardless, we love you as you are right now…so let's learn how to deal with today; the rest will follow in its natural course. Divine Guidance and Deliverance…came to me through strength and faith in that Presence; where He would take us from this hard part…I trusted Him to take us along. I trusted where he would take us. I felt no need to make demands on His plan for our lives; others often did. Our ways are not God's ways. Prayers are answered; sometimes the answer is "no, not that way." What then…?

Or…denial; that this can't be…possibly confused with the power of positive thinking…I would lay down on a table in surgery RIGHT NOW and give Scott my spinal cord if that were possible, but it's not. It is so important to accept what is, what can't be…that doesn't mean giving up on what cures may lie ahead…but there is today, there are so many tomorrows. What will be done with those in the meantime, while waiting for The Cure? Nothing will be done quickly…there is no time to waste. Even patiently waiting for the attendant, the driver, the phone call, etc…is an exercise in learning. Waiting for a reality is different from waiting for an unknown "fix." One is full of planning; the other is only floating in time…the landing in some distant time, possibly never. Read, Talk, Make Phone Calls, Find a Group, Do Something to Learn How to Deal With Paralysis; don't let your loved one make this trip alone. Accept. Yes, it's hard and it hurts…and most of all, it is so frightening. Educating yourself and involvement makes it less so.

Before Scott got out of rehab, Rachel had told him that Peggy had said if I moved back to Greenville to be close to him, she was leaving. Of course, Scott eventually told me. That seemed strange to me as Peggy and I had always more or less accepted each other…that she would make such a comment under these circumstances didn't make any sense to me. I hesitated to try and talk to her about it as I couldn't figure where that was coming from, so I just let it be…and waited. I wasn't going to stay away from

Scott because Peggy might leave; but on the other hand, I still had no desire to interfere in Jim and Peggy's marriage. Jim and Peggy...Rachel...Roger, Beth, Mom, Eileen...so many others who deserved consideration, and I tried...but my only consideration really was Scott. If push came to shove...I'd do what I felt was best for my son, regardless.

When I went up in October to visit Scott; he was in his new home. I looked forward to our first real visit, not in a hospital, since his accident. I hadn't realized...the terrain of where his home was sitting until I got there. Jim's property had a lane turning off the main rural road. It was flat for a distance, then curved up a hill to where Jim and Peggy's house was...on top of the hill, flat. Scott's trailer was set in the middle of the hill between the main road and the top of the hill. There was no driveway, there was a hill behind the trailer that continued its downward slope in front of the trailer. Both ends...the slope of the hill. There was no sidewalk...only rough grass, dirt (potential mud) and The Hill. When I'd read my Parent and Patient's Guide, the "going home" and accessibility part had described nothing like what I saw. Even the door handles were wrong; my brother, Tuny, corrected those later on, changing the knobs to handles that Scott could open himself eventually.

This was October in Illinois...ugly, cold, wet, muddy winter months were rapidly approaching. If a crisis occurred, an emergency vehicle could not have gotten to Scott in the midst of bad weather, and he could not have gotten his chair out to the road to get into it! It was just purely awful. Emphasis on that possibility as while I was there, Scott ended up back in the hospital; had to be taken to St. Louis. He had an internal cyst in his buttock that was infected and had to be removed. So instead of time with him in his home, once more I was spending time with him at the hospital; this time driving back and forth each day. At the hospital, I had to ask Jim when he thought a driveway could be put in so Scott wouldn't be trapped in the middle of The Hill.

When I walked into Scott's new home, I found him covered in a red and white quilt my mom had made for him, still shivering as he had while in St. Louis. When we finally had a few minutes of quiet time together, we had a "hard" talk; one of the few times that Scott "bottomed out" with me. Here he was, 5-6 months into this injury and still feeling God Awful. Shivering just as he had back at the rehab hospital, unable to be up and about even in his wheelchair. I could understand, just didn't want him to give up and wasn't sure at this point at all of how to encourage him. We were all more than ready for SOME PROGRESS, and it didn't seem any was coming our way. His home was lovely, spacious…but the wrong kind of door handles, no roll in shower, a terrible location (Ah but there was already a septic tank, more economical to place it there! The expense was the thing…not those other considerations. Excuse me!)

We ended up first going to the Emergency Room in Greenville where our dear Dr. Daisy (who had come to Greenville as a young, new doctor when I was first pregnant with Scott, so had delivered my 8 lb. 14 oz. 21" son in 1963) examined Scott. He gave us his opinion (which proved correct) but encouraged us to head for St. Louis as neither his expertise nor the examining equipment available in Greenville's excellent but smaller hospital would provide the resources Scott needed. So Scott, Rachel and myself headed for St. Louis. Rachel drove the pick-up truck with Scott inside; I followed in my car.

After endless stupid tests, they finally did what Dr. Daisy had diagnosed in the first place, and he was taken into surgery. Along with everything else, we were learning that doctors can't read charts! If we saw three doctors, we had to go through the same question and answer routine with EACH ONE OF THEM, one right after the other. If we saw five or more, same thing; one couldn't help but wonder why they asked in the first place if no one was writing it down so others could read it! But, they finally figured it out, thankfully. Realize, Scott could not feel pain...even the surgery was done without anesthetics...Sweating, chills, discomfort mean "pain" as we know it to those who are paralyzed; specifically, quads. I have less knowledge of the effects of paralysis on paraplegics. He immediately felt better after the pressure and infection was removed surgically; but during all this and afterward, he was having a terrible time with sinus drainage. Roger had seen the effects of this earlier...during his time with Scott after Hell Week, after I had returned to Orlando.

We able-bodied people, even those of us who smoke so normally deal with the hacking and coughing that accompany our bad habit...or those of us who deal with allergies, so also cough and hack and sneeze...have no conception of how it would be NOT TO BE ABLE to give a big, hard cough...or sneeze...that clears our air passages. I had seen his "sneezes" and had asked, what was that? Obviously, something had happened…his eyes squeezed shut for a moment and his head pitched forward a bit, but that was pretty much it. What was that? No more hearty Ah-Choo's…with dishes rattling in the cupboard or the curtains flapping in the breeze created. Now, just eyes squeezed tightly together for a moment…a very small if any choo! Well, that's not so bad…but what about those times when there is all that goop in one's chest and even with the best of lungs and chest muscles, it's hard to get it Up and Out?…and this was at the hospital, with Scott laying on his back in bed, slightly elevated…Harder still. When he's up in his chair, it's some easier…but this was still during the "early" part. He wasn't up in his chair and as active as he was later to become routinely. This really was as hard for me to see as the first transfer had been…worse in a way because I knew the transfer was to be dealt with, not necessarily distressful to Scott…but this inability to cough up congestion was…

It remains a problem to be dealt with; but realize that in the days ahead when our loved one is upright and more active, the problem is alleviated to a larger degree. Everyone who is hospitalized, for surgery or other events, is very quickly gotten up and out of bed and ambulatory once more, to keep the lungs clear. It goes without saying then that our loved ones who are paralyzed can't just get up and around…so any congestion that accumulates can't help but be a part of the initial health problem or discomfort. This is strictly my theory…for what it's worth and from what I've seen as Scott progressed. No one reassured me or informed me of such at the time…doubtful that Scott understood either...I think it would have helped at least to know it wouldn't always be this difficult when his sinuses were draining. Under saner, safer circumstances, we probably would have realized ourselves, but I must repeat ALL THESE FIRST TIMES were so frightening.

Still, in spite of the difficulties that had been a part of that visit, I came back to Orlando knowing Scott was stronger and with that, realized even more how very fragile he had been during all the previous visits. We had all been so intent on thinking "tomorrow" and "getting through this and into that..." and we were totally ignorant of what/how things really were. That knowledge accentuated all that Scott had already determined, managed to do...it was a bittersweet moment of recognition.

Realizing the progress that had been made and the strength that had gained also finally allowed a time for grieving. The worst of it was over. He was going to make it. With that sense of faith and hope, the reality could now be faced...and I felt the "loss" of my son. Scott was now my "new" son, and he was just as dear and I loved him just as much...but I had lost the Scott who had been, and the time had come to quietly and privately deal with my feelings over that.

By this time (4 months + post-Hell Week), there weren't so many telephone calls; it was quieter when I came back from Illinois...quieter when I'd come in from work during the week. My mind wrestled with, "But Scott is alive, how could you tell anyone you'd lost your son...They wouldn't understand." * But I had lost him...my Scott who would put up my clothesline, mow my grass, fix things so easily, fuss over the toilet paper not being soft enough, who had to lower his head to be able to walk through the door into my trailer, who played ball, picked me up at the airport in St. Louis when I'd go up to visit my family and who always made the trip so easy for me (no one in Greenville liked to drive into St. Louis, except Scott), etc. All those visual, physical things...They were gone, and how I missed all of them. Now you see them; now you don't except I had to wait...four months to cry...and cry...and cry some more. When Scott had gone to Pakistan to work, I didn't think he could ever get further away from me; I would find myself then wishing he was still in Pakistan. Why did I ever want him to come home...to this? All the plans and excitement and successes led to this? How can this be?

*October 11, 1992. Months after Scott's accident, others who had graduated from the High School Jim and I had attended in Greenville lost their son, Doug, who was about Scott's age in an accident; empathetic to such a loss, I wrote to them about how sorry I was to hear of their son's death. Carolyn wrote back with deepest sincerity and loving intent that at least their sorrow had an ending. If this had been a direct conversation, eye to eye, I don't think I could have taken the consolation as intended even though I knew that was absolutely the intent...I don't know how I would have/could have handled it. Pre-accident, that would have been my thought, I knew what she meant...but I was smack in the middle of trying to let go, forget...and trying to accept and continue with the old love for this new son. Then, here in black and white before my eyes...I didn't know whether to give into the suffering forever after which was inferred or write back that how dare she or anyone ever think it was better to lose their child forever? There were those differing truths…again…This time, hers and mine, two mothers…both allowed. We both wanted to comfort the other…In that, there was no conflict of perception.

I was so lonesome for Scott, the old Scott. How could I stop missing him? I knew I had to find a way. My new Scott couldn't be wholly accepted as he now was if I couldn't let go of the old Scott. I hoped these times were healthy and meant a healing could occur; and I think that is what happen was happening. It was a very hurtful time, but I don't think I could have come to be as comfortable or as accepting of present circumstances if I had not gone through those emptying-out times…alone. Quietly. Wholly. The past had held such full and alive times, such a reinforcement of what I had hoped to present to the world through my efforts as a parent. Scott had been re-born, and I hadn't known I was pregnant! I had never ever thought of how I would provide parenting to a child in a wheelchair, a quadriplegic. I had never ever thought of how I would help teach or support such a child. Please know, Scott was not a "child" when this happened nor did he behave as a "child" after the accident, just to this mother…and I think to all mothers…in our hearts, our children from the time of their wondrous birth to our death…remain our "children/child." I saw that when my father's mother who was in her 90's died, and Dad was certainly "old" himself by that time…more than anything else at that funeral, I knew Grandma's little boy was now without his mother and was so full of hurt from the loss, like a child. Grandma's child; my father. That thought for all of us since has remained so precious to me. At a time when I thought I had gotten my firstborn child through to independence; it suddenly wasn't true at all and the parent in me searched for ways to help her child.

While in Greenville, I had been surprised to hear Rachel say she wanted to come to Florida, too. Scott and I had talked about it; I absolutely felt there were resources here that that weren't available in Greenville or even St. Louis that we could find. But Scott was so dependent on Rachel and trusted her choices and decisions, I was not comfortable with presenting different views on most options. My surprise stemmed mainly from Rachel's resentment of any interference from me, or others. I was so pleased that she was willing to consider, even encourage a move to Orlando. So, with that realization, I did have that hoped for possibility working its way through my mind.

Adjustments had to be made to my trailer (as anyone could well imagine) before Scott could "get in" much less anything else that needed consideration. I got in touch with Marvin Vessels, one of the superintendents from LeCesse Corporation where I had worked before Parsons Brinckerhoff. Marvin is one of those rough and tough and grumbly people with a heart of gold…as is often found in the dust and dirt of all those construction crews you see building highways, bridges, buildings, airports. He built the ramp on my screened in porch for a fraction of what it would have cost me if done by others, and I haven't forgotten his kindness and hard work. How could I ever? There wasn't enough room (length) to do it at the proper slant, but at least Scott could GET IN, and he took the little piece of wall off from the bedroom door and the door that led into my bedroom at the end of the hall so his chair would fit through the opening. Scott would have to use my bedroom as it was the only one large enough for his wheelchair to move about in at all. Thereafter, I bought a folding screen to place across the opening for privacy when desired. By January, 1992, I was ready…but still, couldn't really believe it could happen…1,000 miles in a wheelchair, no van with a lift…but if Scott and Rachel could find a way, I was ready for them and they would find themselves so welcomed in Orlando.

His physical stability remained a potential threat for any plans…"something" was always happening. Also, shortly after he had left critical care at St. Lukes and was in "rehab" in St. Louis, I had been given enough information to realize there were likely insurance problems. Scott was not in a position to be fully involved in what was happening around him; Jim was most directly involved in those processes. Eventually, we all learned that instead of the medical insurance Scott had believed he had through his employer in fact did not exist at all, as his employer had failed to keep up the insurance premiums for his employees. His employer's insurance had been cancelled by the insurance company prior to Scott's accident and was not in effect. Regardless of that, his employer did commit to being personally responsible for all Scott's medical bills…but however fully his intent to do so (or his desire to cover his backside), it would of course prove to be too large an order for one man, especially one who in a few short months would find himself in bankruptcy court.

In the area of expenses incurred by a spinal cord injury, even moderate wealth falls way short of the funds necessary to keep up with the bills. But time was going by, Scott was getting on…with many things considering. He managed to get a letter from that employer to give to Humana Lucerne in Orlando which stated he would be responsible for Scott's expenses there and at Normandy Manor, the center for independent living which was adjacent to Humana.

Even though concerned about the costs and Mr. Employer's ability regarding payments, I wanted Scott to have all the benefits available in Orlando, to be a part of a group that could share their experiences with him, show him what could be in months to come. Their presence in my life had made all the difference; I was sure it would do the same for Scott as it had for so many before him. To get him to Orlando so he could be a part of all this, was my constant hope and dream. Scott had a new life to get on with and needed all the help he could get to learn how to do that. I didn't care about any other consequences. Whatever, however…it just had to be done if possible and the time had to be used wisely in case it didn't last.

Through November, I had continued to avoid going out, doing things Scott could no longer do…being with friends beyond the confines of our homes or at the office…to go "out," really talk with or get acquainted with others…I could not. From another direction, I could not put on others the pain I was feeling in myself. I could not pull out of the world in which Scott was the center.

Roger and I had always been so very close. He was being so wonderful with Scott...he and Beth were continuing to be the close and loving couple; progressing toward wedding plans, and I could not have been happier for them...or about the young woman Roger had chosen to share his life with...but my heart held nothing but concern for Scott. He was all there was during these hard, hard times. I just kept thanking God that Roger was well and had Beth. I felt I was letting him down, but Scott's needs were so great...and I still didn't know how or when or if or...I was just totally involved in that and constantly available, open to a need or a call or whatever. And it wasn't just meeting "new" people that I feared putting my pain on...After a while, if I had not kept up with old friends, I would just avoid them...too much to catch up on or explain...too painful to backtrack and tell about the events of the past several months.

Parsons Brinckerhoff had given me...the contact and resources available at Humana through Mel Kohn's daughter, Robin; time away from work to be with Scott in Illinois when I needed to be; a secure job when I needed it most of all; and a friend, Steve Mix, who pulled me out of that lost place and made me get involved once more in the life still going on around me in December. What a good, decent guy...and special friend he was/is. We went out to dinner, to movies...it was all right. Scott didn't resent it...and Steve wasn't depressed by me because of the situation in our lives; neither was he uncomfortable meeting Scott later on when Scott still had miles to go in rehabilitation and increased strength. Yes, Scott did get to Orlando in 1992. What joy accompanied his entry into this trailer that I call home. Steve now works away from the Orlando area, still with Parsons Brinckerhoff. We are not in touch often, but this special man deserves a very happy and secure future, at least equal to if not more than the one he has helped me to continue for myself. Without realizing it, I had so needed his reinforcement that this was "all right" to go on living wholly and happily.

CHAPTER FOUR

From Illinois to Florida Etc.!

January, 1992...after the 1st and before my 48th birthday on the 24th...You'd think I would remember the exact date, but I don't. But one night, Scott's Mustang with Rachel behind the wheel of the car packed to the max pulled into the driveway next door. No one was living there, and it was easier to get Scott out on that side. Scott had always liked his Skoal, so Rachel had taped a plastic cup to his hand and had put that pinch between his cheek and gum for him...besides the "humor" in that, there was an extra bonus along on the trip...Blade, a black pit bull pup, cute at that size! Scott has always had his "special dog," so this seemed right although I felt sorry for Rachel...thought she had her hands full with Scott, much less a dog also. Only "the young" think they can do anything, God Bless Them...and Rachel was young when she found herself in love with a quadriplegic who had been Mr. Independent Sports Star when she first started dating him. Anyway, I CANNOT think about what that drive must have been like for the three of them. As I've said, it was just too good to be true that he was there...my mind couldn't think of how it had been getting there!

I tried to give Scott and Rachel their time alone and privacy. I was at work during the day and I'd spend time at Steve's in the evenings sometimes. I didn't want to get on their nerves, and I didn't want them to get on mine…company and the "old fish story" usually proves true…and I wasn't sure how this would all play out.   Scott had to wait to get in for a check-up at Humana to see what the next step would be, and that took longer than we'd thought it would. A lot, if not most, of Scott's time here (this time…) was spent on the couch…he still had that original spot on his butt; as I'm trying to recall at this distant place in time, it seems they had finally done some repair work on it in St. Louis. Scott and Rachel had been led to believe it was healing nicely, but he was still trying to keep off his butt until it was 100%; aside from that, he wasn't feel real well regardless, probably because of the spot on his rear end but we didn't realize that possibility for a while.

Our friends, the Sklareks, came up and had dinner with us one day; Roger and Beth were here also; Steve was here one night for dinner and to meet my kids. Scott and Rachel made a few day trips to see other old friends of Scott's.   They had dinner at Roger and Beth's one evening.   The ramp Marvin built worked…but I realized I needed to do something to create a rougher surface on it. Scott was able to get in and out…but both were with effort; coming in, to get up the ramp…going out, to get down safely without going through the end of the screened in porch! Eventually, I added some sand to the paint to roughen the surface which helped some, but there was nothing I could do about the height. At this point, he was still in a manual chair so it proved pretty much up to Rachel's muscle power to make sure he was able to get in or out. With all the practice she had from transfers, she needed no other work-outs to keep in shape. Once outside, the roots from the tree in my front yard didn't prove to be any more forgiving to a wheelchair than they did to my lawn mower! (Wouldn't you know, that same special brother of mine would later come down and remove those, just like he had replaced the door handles in Illinois for Scott...The roots have grown back by this time; perhaps I can get him to come back for another visit!)

The minor adjustments to my bedroom at the end of the hall worked out all right. In that room, the bath is fairly open at the end of the trailer, so Scott could get up to the sink, but as it had a cabinet under it...not very close, just workable if you really wanted it to "work" and we did...most of the time!

I would go to bed in my smaller guest room off the hall earlier than Scott and Rachel. Helped me catch up on some of my reading, and I had a radio in there. One night, Blade was scratching and whining outside my bedroom door, so I let him in. He and I had become "buds"; he was still small enough to be a lap dog and often, when I was sitting at my counter mornings, having my coffee, writing a letter or reading, Blade would jump up and scratch on my thighs until I'd pick him up and let him lay in my lap. Then, he'd quiet down nicely...so he usually got his way. I let the "scratching dog" in, and he jumped up on the bed with me, curled up beside me and went to sleep. Later in the night, when Scott and Rachel were going to bed, Rachel came to the door, opened it just enough for Blade to get out and called him...He growled. He was definitely bent on protecting this sleeping lady...but from his "owner," and I couldn't think Rachel would see the humor in that! Dear Blade...we didn't have many really funny moments during those weeks but I still laugh when I think of that night. I just acted like I was sound asleep. The next morning, I privately asked Scott if he'd heard Blade growl at Rachel. He said he had, and he'd thought it was funny…I told him I did, too, but I didn't want Rachel to be upset by it!

All things considered, we managed…and for the most part, well under the circumstances; we had those unpleasant times, of course…even a few down right nasty ones! Rachel's control had been firmly established during the weeks before they came to Orlando…how could it have been otherwise? I had hoped by this time, she would be willing to share the responsibility a bit more, but it hadn't proven to be that way; not that there really was much Roger or I could do to take that load off her shoulders, but we wanted to do what we could, both for her sake and for Scott's. Neither my attempts nor Roger's were well taken…and unfortunately, Scott was the one to get the brunt of her anger. Rachel's contributions and efforts were beyond measure; I will always love her for the time and energy and love she gave to my son. None of that is taken away by the times that were less than kind, less than patient, perhaps less than honest as time went by. We've all had times in life when we've wanted to be totally capable of whatever the challenge happened to be at that time. It's a very difficult lesson to learn; that sometimes we can't be all powerful, all knowing…INDEPENDENTLY able. Both Scott and Rachel were realizing independence vs. dependence; both were learning to be helped while helping.

One of the first warnings I was given by Scott concerning Rachel after he was hurt was that she didn't want me to hug her…My family…we hug…not everybody, but certainly those we love and are happy to see, to be with. When he told me, I remembered when I first got to the hospital after he was hurt…from Orlando…in my mind, Rachel was the only one I seemed to see there before I got to Scott…and we hugged each other. I wished that feeling between us had not gotten lost, but it evidently had. Other warnings, "Mom, Rachel doesn't want you to…" followed. It really never got easier…

Scott finally got into Humana for his check-up. While there, he met John from the support group who I had told him about. He and Rachel were as I had been; watching him, it was hard to KNOW John was quadriplegic. So, although they got hard news from the doctor after Scott's examination, thankfully meeting John had provided that hoped for motivation in spite of a break in the middle of plans. Scott was told the place on his butt was NOT healing, that it never would heal as it was, could only worsen. He needed surgery on it, which would mean time in bed…weeks. Scott realizing his limited funds, decided under the circumstances it would be best to go back to Greenville to have the surgery and to recuperate. This was the FIRST personal confirmation of my firmly held beliefs in what Orlando could offer that was not offered by service and treatment previously available during the first seven-plus months post-injury. Many others would follow, but they would have to wait. I shudder to think what would have happened if Scott hadn't gotten down here…just for that, if nothing else…to see Humana's doctor and find out what was really happening with the broken down skin on his butt. We read and are told about skin breakdowns, but continue to trust the "professionals..." and unless they truly have the expertise, they are just like the rest of us...only "scholars" without real knowledge. One wouldn't take his Porsche to the John Deere dealer for service; likewise, spinal cord injuries should not be treated by any staff or facility where spinal cord injuries are not the specialty of the house, or hospital as it were.

Scott was in excellent hands with Dr. Krettek at St. Lukes West who knew Scott prior to his spinal injury, having done back surgery on him two times prior to that. The acute care facility at St. Lukes West was wonderful; all that followed, I can't say anyone did "wrong"; they just didn't know how to do "right." I can give you a long, long list of names of people and staff, who I truly liked and trusted to "care" for their patient, my son, after St. Lukes; but they didn't have the expertise I found when I visited Humana in Orlando. That "spot" had been there since practically the beginning of his "rehabilitation" in St. Louis...that it took Humana to identify it correctly is a perfect example of the difference in care offered.

Aside from Dr. Krettek, I trusted Dr. Daisy most...our beloved general practitioner in little old Greenville; what he may have lacked in expertise, he more than made up for in care and sincere personal interest. He had delivered Scott into this world; he cared what was happening to Scott Alan Darnell. To Dr. Daisy, Scott wasn't just patient # 77674. He had diagnosed what was wrong with Scott when the cyst was present, even without tests, tests and more tests. If

I had doubted him before (and I didn't), I believed in him even more after that.

Valentine's Day, 1992 or the day after, Scott and Rachel returned to Greenville; Scott to have his surgery, heal and eventually, return to Orlando...sights still set on Humana and Normandy Manor. I think I just waited...no trips to Illinois for me for quite a while.

When Scott had been with me here before he went to Illinois (he had always done that; live here in Florida; then missing his dad, he would go to Illinois for a while...only to eventually return to Florida), he had left me walking tall. When he came back, he rolled through the door in his wheelchair, but regardless, there had been joy in his arrival. Getting here was the hard part; the new path had begun. Scott was on his way back. Differently, but he was on his way back to life even though he had to leave Florida again to get ready for it.

There were things that happened throughout all these months and later that I can no longer put in order of any kind; they are jumbled memories or stories I was only told about because I wasn't there. His first fall out of the wheelchair (I told him we'd learned then that he wasn't so very fragile after all) on that durned monster hill around his trailer; getting down on the floor while being transferred (Jim had to come down and help with that); the TV antennae and tractor star wars episode with Scott inside wondering what hell had broken loose outside his new home, the scarred siding then that served to remind everyone of the scare; the purchase of a van and the addition of a ramp to the van; more colds and sinus problems, repeated urinary tract infections; going to a basketball game with his cousins in Champagne, Illinois; his returns to our little church in the country in Greenville, with my mama sitting nearby, being with them once more for communion which is held in June every year; the high school quarterback returning to the high school football games in his wheelchair; mastering the Skoal can on his own.

Mid-May 1992, he finally got back to Orlando; his butt healed…ready to begin at Humana. Before he was even settled in, they were telling him how they would get his neck muscles straightened so his head wouldn't be pushed forward!!! That was corrected quickly…and with that, his balance was much improved. Scott's roommate at Humana was Russell, a paraplegic high school senior from Tavares, Florida, who attended his graduation ceremony with his other classmates on a day pass from rehab less than two months after his accident. Frankie, his mother, and I exchanged recipes; I gave her Spaghetti Stroganoff (which I'd taken into Scott one night and shared with them). She gave me Spaghetti Pie which I still make, so think of Russell and his warm family every time I enjoy it.

If I remember correctly, it was during this time that Scott and Rachel had gone to one of the peer group meetings and finally met others who had been supremely important to me, and to Roger and Beth who had gone often with me also. This group educated, encouraged and created the platform from which everything else came.

In addition to those in wheelchairs and Robin, the counselor, there was John's mother, Gay. She lived in

California and while visiting John in Orlando, came to one of the meetings. I have been blessed through life with GOOD friends; but none are more treasured than Gay. We didn't talk a lot at that meeting, but I felt I would like to know her better. At the next month's meeting, I asked for her address. I think it was just before Easter that year ('92), and I sent her an Easter card with just a short note in it. And there began the exchange of "manuscripts" between the two of us. We were both mothers of quadriplegics we were so proud of, as well as other children who filled our hearts so fully. Financially, Gay and I lived in different worlds; I knew that and when I sent her the card, could not have imagined what lay in store for the two of us. I have her to thank for so very much; as much love as she certainly gave her children, she so generously also shared with me.

I have encouraged those of you reading this who have personal tragedy you are dealing with to LEARN, READ, EDUCATE yourself about the spinal cord injury, or whatever your situation may be. That, to help the one who is in distress. For your own personal pain or distress as relates to that, if you can find your own "Gay," your progress and optimism will increase one-hundred fold. Just as those in the peer group could identify with each other; you need to find that OTHER who is like you...someone who understands YOU; someone you can understand and trust to be open with. Others (as a parent, as a brother or sister, as a friend) who haven't really "been there" help tremendously, but that ONE who has been can be a real lifeline to hang onto. Half of what I went through was devotion to Scott's progress; to have that half to give him, I was so fortunate to find the other half that re-stocked my own stamina and determination. I hope you do also.

Scott had returned and was settled into Humana in Orlando, but with Scott's return to Illinois earlier, Roger and Beth had set a date. Beth was going to become Roger's wife and my daughter-in-law. We couldn't know at the time when Scott would be coming back, and they had set the date for May 23; to be held at our little country church (Mt. Nebo) in Illinois (thinking Scott would still be there and would be Roger's best man). It was MOST EXCELLENT that Scott was back in Orlando to begin his real rehabilitation; it was MOST EXCELLENT that Roger and Beth were getting married in our little church in Illinois, but I was so torn. Before we left for Illinois, Roger and Beth had a pre-wedding party in Orlando for friends here that Scott was able to attend. I think Roger picked him up at Humana and took him, but his trip back...was with another quad, our pretty little Donna from the group. Donna was another quad who was well on her way to recovery. We were all still at the hard part, and it definitely lifted our spirits that two quads were together; one of them driving the other back to his "home," just like other regular able-bodied drivers with passengers. It didn't matter that the equipment they had to do that with (van/lift/etc.) wasn't the more stylish sports car with bucket seats, although Donna's van was definitely stylish, a black and pink model! Hooray! Great goin', Scott!

We left Scott in Orlando and the rest of us were in Illinois with all the families, ours/Beth's from Florida, Wisconsin...enjoying the very special occasion together, except for Scott, but we all understood the priorities. Both my sons were at beginning places…I just couldn't be with both of them at the same time. For Roger's wedding, I had to be there, and it was beautiful. Roger's father filled in for Scott as his best man. Roger's cousin, Bart, was two months younger than Roger and the two had always been close, but Bart and Bobbie were expecting their first child and didn't live in Greenville. We didn't know if Bart could be there or not. Bobbie cooperated, little KayeLee arrived early the morning of the 23rd and Bart was at the wedding. I had talked with Scott back in Orlando earlier in the day. He dictated something to me for Bart to read for him at the reception after the wedding.

Roger and Beth packed all their beautiful wedding gifts, including her gown, into the back of my car. If I didn't already have added incentive to get back to Orlando in a hurry, that did it for sure! Everyone understood so as soon as I could, I was driving south (17 hours of driving). Even at the reception, it was hard to relax…I didn't stay long. I took Mom home and was content to stay with her. I didn't think I'd be missed but both Roger and Beth have talked about it since. I wish I had stayed; I was so happy and sad at the same time…I just couldn't.

I had called the paper in Osceola County where Scott had gone to school, played ball, had friends…We'd lived in St. Cloud most of the years before high school, and Scott had continued to be in touch with friends there. I asked the paper to run a personal ad regarding Scott's temporary residence in rehab at Humana and that he would enjoy seeing old friends. One of the reporters called me back and asked if they could interview Scott, do an article. I was afraid they wouldn't do an upbeat report, but I told them I appreciated their interest. I also told them I'd have to check with Scott first and see what his reaction was. As usual, Scott was open to everything and the article by Amy J. Ellis in the paper was great. The photographer, Scott Fisher, had caught it all...the effort, the smiling face, the determination and hope. He later sent me some extra copies and a note. That issue of the Osceola News-Gazette was dated June 6, 1992.

Scott went back to Greenville after he left Humana, before he became a resident of Normandy Manor. That was when he got his van and the ramp added. There were no modifications yet for his being able to drive; Rachel was still his chauffeur. I had made a note in October of '92, that Scott had told me he would see himself in the mirror and be surprised because he'd forget that he was in a wheelchair. He was in his home in Greenville when he told me that. I told myself if Scott could forget, then I could, too. It was such a comfort knowing that he could; it's what I would want to happen, I just didn't know if it could ever be that way for anyone in that situation. No one else had ever told me they "forgot."

The time came when Scott did move into Normandy Manor; his roommate would be Adam. At Normandy Manor, for the first time...Scott was alone. There were attendants coming in throughout the day and during the night (to turn him), but he would for the most part, be ALONE. He and Adam each had their own bedrooms. If Scott had trouble during the night, who would help him? Adam was another quad, but of smaller build and lighter weight; he was able to transfer himself in and out of his chair. That first night I don't know if Scott was as "concerned" as I was...but, I just kept telling myself, see how things are tomorrow. Just like falling out of the chair, this was another "first" although certainly a safer one. We started having more of those. The frustrations felt back in October/November were lessening with each additional "first." The first night went well.

Roger and Beth brought in their typewriter. Bill Saravanja from Parsons and I brought in concrete blocks that Bill contributed to the "cause"; Roger brought a board to be used as a desktop. Scott proved to be an excellent typist; just slower than he had been before, but the lack of speed was made up for in the increase in accuracy. He was able to lock one thumb into a position that enabled him to use the keyboard. Of course with his successes in this, we were all excited about a computer for him to use at some point in the future.

We were all able to visit more often with Scott here. Roger and Beth would often ride their bicycles over. I would do Scott's laundry for him; occasionally cook for him. Adam had been an executive chef prior to his injury, which was a bit intimidating to me! But Adam was a great sport about that and everything else. I was as pleased with Scott's roommate as Scott was. Adam left Normandy Manor before Scott did...he called me a few times afterward, but we've since lost him and haven't been able to find him since. (Adam, if you're out there and read this...or if you're someone who knows Adam...please let us know how you are, where you are and all the rest. We miss you.) Scott and I had a quiet Thanksgiving dinner together at

Normandy. Not like any other before…but surely with even more blessings than others we had enjoyed.

It is so important and something I tried to protect Rachel from…to honestly find one's limit in what one has time and energy to do and what has to be set aside or left for others. It serves no one to TRY SO HARD that there is no energy left over for anything else. I knew I couldn't BE Scott, so save him from anything. This new life, he would have to figure out on his own; I trusted his ability to do it…and as always, knew he would do it well. I knew I couldn't get tired and not admit it. I asked him for his honesty in what he needed. We worked on what schedule would work best for both of us…eventually, working it out to every 3rd, 4th or 5th day…Then, when I was there, I was really there, ready to do for him…not thinking about the things and time I needed to do chores for myself. Scott had the grocery shopping down to a science. He would give me his list and know almost to the exact penny how much it all was going to cost.

Perhaps I don't have the stamina others do, physically or emotionally, but it is impossible to have so much put on the care provider for the long haul. There must be shared efforts…or Burn Out has to occur. It can't be helped. There is the injured one who most certainly wants to have that ONE he or she can trust totally, who privacy can be maintained with to provide all physical needs and assist with personal care…Understandable; even the answer to a prayer, but there comes a price with that. A loving relationship vs. a medical attendant; Patient and devoted parents with a kind and thoughtful "child" vs. stressed parents with a young adult who is totally self-centered…or who carries a huge feeling of guilt because regardless of his or her need, there is a realization of what is being "sacrificed" by others for him or her. One person can't be ALL. We have to help each other; and the one we want to help has to LET US. The time will come that the help won't be so necessary. If we're real, real lucky, by the time we get there, we'll still like each other a lot! Got to work at it though; so hard to say "I'm sorry, I can't…" when you really want to with all your heart. That will be accepted and respected though, and there will be no guilt or resentment silently building in the meantime.

I had dreaded the approach of June 29, 1992, the anniversary of Scott's accident. I had thought it would be an awful, depressing day. Every day since June 29, 1991, there had been that remembrance of how things had been "last year": birthdays, visits, celebrations, travels, visits, work, sports, fun, adventures, plans. When it came, I was pleasantly surprised and relieved. Instead, I found that from that "dreaded" date, we could look back at "last year" and realize the progress that had been made…I thought of Robin and how right she had been after all. It had "gotten easier" although I can't tell you the number of times I had asked myself "how can it?" in between. On June 29, 1991, Scott had been a breath away from death. How much we had to be thankful for one year later! We were making it. Scott was getting there. That was my frame of mind during that quiet Thanksgiving together at Normandy Manor. There was no other place or no other person I would have preferred spending that day with. I had ever so much to be thankful for.

While at Normandy, Scott had the procedure to have a Suprapubic catheter placed, which is a tube inserted in the bladder through an opening in the skin in the lower abdomen that allows urine to drain from the bladder. Urinary tract infections happen; less so with the Suprapubic. He also had a skin graft done on one of his heels that kept breaking down and slowed his progress while there. Before Normandy, while there and afterward, there have been burns: from a hot sandwich on his hand, from a space heater on his legs. There have been more falls, not A LOT but some: once when he'd forgotten he had his wheelie bars up…bounced back to get over a door jamb and didn't stop. All the way over…Skin breakdowns continue to occur fairly often on his heels from shoes or socks not being put on properly…Unfortunate when this happens, but then we think of how much worse it would be if it were on his butt like before…and how that would really slow him down. If he must have an unusually vulnerable area for skin breakdown, I suppose his heels are about the best place to have it. The WORST was truly over by the time he got to Normandy, but there are always concerns and hazards others can't even be aware of. Still, it gets better…day-by-day.

After Normandy, Scott returned to Greenville once more. Time had proven these 1,000 miles between the two states wouldn't keep him away; and financially, it seemed to make more sense for him to do that. When he went back that time, he was READY to get ready for "tomorrow." He'd had to come to Normandy and find some semblance of independence once more before he could do that, but he was READY when he left. This time, coming down and going back, he was in his chair in his van…not stuffed into the bucket seat of a Ford Mustang with all the clothes and medical supplies and a dog! When he left Normandy Manor, Scott's cousin, Joel, had come down from Illinois to do the driving. Rachel had always been along on such trips…but she, too, was getting life back in gear. She'd re-enrolled in college, but was there waiting when Scott got back to Greenville.

Both had had a healthy taste of renewed independence…a break in the chain of dependence. They both needed that space between each other to take a closer look at themselves and their futures, whether together or apart. It wasn't time to decide or know that yet, but it had been right that they had that time apart, a gentle nudge that began when he first went into Humana, then reinforced with time spent at Normandy. Although Rachel still was there and helped, Scott had determined to find attendant care separate from that Rachel had always provided. He wanted the relationship with her, not the attendant care from her, and wanted to take the responsibility part off her shoulders as much as he could.

In May '93, Roger and I went to Greenville. Mother's Day for me with my sons (a bonus being the miles together on the road, time for me and Roger to catch up on so much)…for me and my Mama. I have photos of me and Scott from that trip…he'd borrowed a powerchair to check out. Had just gotten it just before Roger and I got there. Up until this, we'd only seen him in his manual chair…and although we admired his determination to push himself and gain strength in that exercise, it was like a breath of fresh air to see him in that power chair going across the rough grass so easily...his hair blowing in the breezes! So many things required so much effort, it was just wonderful to see him easily GO wherever. So, I hoped to promote that in the near future; but that, like everything had to come (or go) in Scott's own sweet time. Good...that's how it should be. Also, although Scott had his van with him at Normandy, I never took him anywhere in it; so I didn't drive it until that trip to Illinois. It was like old times seeing Roger and Scott pull up in the driveway at Mom's. Scott was finally well enough and strong enough and had the transportation to be able to go places again. That's where the photo was taken. There is a creek down the road from Mom's that the road crosses over. Scott and I went down to the bridge together. I had visited that creek, gone to that bridge so many times as a child either alone or with others in the family and with my sons after they were born; Scott and Roger had played in that same creek so many times as they were growing up. When he was about 10 or 12, he had found an arrow head there on one of his adventures along the creek bank that I had bought from him before he could sell it to anyone else! But on that day so many years after both our childhoods, I had on a St. Louis Cardinals shirt he had given me; he was in his powerchair. We were coming/going like we used to; the difference being I was using my legs while Scott was using his wheels. It was wonderful. He still had to wait for someone else to drive him, which Roger was tickled to death to do (and which Rachel usually did sans transfers now) but much progress was being made, in many ways.

Scott also got his computer that trip. That was one of Roger's jobs! The computer setter upper! He's so good at that, among so many other things and is well established as our family computer expert and so patient with all our requests and needs! Since the typewriter at Normandy, and the computer in May '93, Scott has now progressed to graphics and done some wonderful drawings on his computer (1997). Most of all though, I've enjoyed his writings...Whether deserved or not, I like to think we have my father to thank for this gift of writing. Dad's bent toward writing limericks, slogans and songs (like My Darlin' Lulu) and Primitive Baptist Church philosophy MUST have been his gift to me that I have been fortunate to have gotten to share with my sons. To me, it couldn't have come from anyone else...

Through life...book reports and compositions in school, then to letters to friends and family from wherever we were living at the time, and then in poetry or in journals that helped me find myself more honestly...attempts at novels...always some kind of writing had been my companion. Roger went more directly toward that goal, preparing himself in college to be "a writer..." and then Scott, when he found himself beyond the water sports and basketball courts, baseball fields...beautifully presented his feelings and experiences in words, taking it further even...into art works. Communication...in whatever form it takes...and Expression...the freedom and courage to express. Take these away from us, what would we be? How could we be?

Those with disabilities are more aware of "barriers" than the rest of us as we come and go in this busy world of the 1990s. How many places do you go to that you first must find out if you can physically get into or not? How many times have you looked at those "prime" handicapped parking spaces and been a little irritated by the "conveniences" they are allowed? Next time, picture yourself in a wheelchair that comes out of the van on a lift that takes 3-5 feet of space…plus additional space for the chair to come off from, with turning space then most likely required; the extra wide parking space is not a convenience, it's a real necessity. That's really the simpler of two scenarios; the driver can at least TRY to find a space where there is room for the ramp. The other scenario: Picture yourself coming back to your "conveniently" parked van and some inconsiderate or unknowing other driver has parked so close that there isn't room for the ramp to be lowered, much less your being able to get onto the ramp, so you're blocked OUT. You finally have a vehicle you can drive, but in that situation…you're stuck OUT…can't get in, can't go…and maybe there's a dark cloud up above, and all at once the sky opens up…or…(Get the picture? Good.)

My personal promotion as relates to handicap parking spaces would be more colorful. I think they should be color coded as according to need, and those colors would apply to all the decals on the vehicles as well. Then, those who require space for their ramps would not find themselves blocked out of their vehicles so easily. The one who parked too close doesn't know probably; but then, there are the ones who don't care…Ah, you foolish souls…that you might never realize why you should. However, those standard blue handicap decals and parking spaces make a blanket statement that don't always seem applicable to others. The variances in requirements aren't "standard issue" at all.

Communication and Expression Barriers though are invisible ones we all may be more familiar with. Why communication and expression comes so easily for some and is such a difficult or uncomfortable means of growth for others is not understood by this active communicator. Only by opening up and sharing can we find acceptance; not that others always agree and so "validate" what we have said or written...but that the world doesn't come to an end if they don't! So, this family writes...Myself, Scott, Roger...and Dad, who started it all. Perhaps, his most precious legacy was left behind for his grandson when he began pondering the world while sitting in his wheelchair behind his computer. It allowed all the inside secrets, fears and doubts to be placed on paper for an escape from an inner hell; as well as all the joys, blessings and hopes being released as though helium filled balloons floating up into life's sunshine, taking the writer with them into tomorrow.

I drove the van my first time on this trip up. Always before, Roger and I had been more observers than activists...there for and with Scott, but not really participating with him. This trip was full of all kinds of shared events. For the first time in almost two years!

A ramp had finally been built on the front of Scott's trailer...a large deck out front, then the deck with two landings on it before the third slant finally got him down to the driveway. I don't remember if it was the evening he and I were going out...or another, but at one time or another, he had gotten down to the second landing, and was going down the last one backward in his manual chair. THANK GOD for those wheelie bars...up came his chair, and my mind said to me "Lila, you're going to see your son fall flat on his back NOW...stay calm." Unbelievably, I laugh now as I put it on paper. Scott's wonderful humor...Ah, the wheelie bars caught him and he got re-leveled out in his chair, progressed on down to the driveway. When he was safely planted there, I told him what I'd just expected to happen...he said, "Me, too, Mom." I don't think Scott had been up and down that R-A-M-P much prior to my and Roger being there with him. I thought he was used to that kind of thing happening, and I was trying not to act "like a mother" and there he was, evidently scared a bit shitless, too! (Please pardon my *French*, but sometimes it's the only apt description!) Strange that I can now laugh about it, because while laughing...I still remember how I felt as every bone in my body turned to mush while I was waiting for the "inevitable..."

But the night of our outing, Scott took me out to dinner for Mother's Day. Roger had been born on Thursday before Mother's Day in 1966; then this Mother's Day in 1993, Scott and I going out together again. I'm sure all Mother's celebrate this day in their hearts each year; but surely, I more than most. Okay, we're in the van. Scott in his chair behind the driver's seat, all locked in place...we're set, and I'm telling myself I can do this. I consider myself to be a fairly good "backer upper" and in times past, I've done a fine job of even backing a trailer with a boat on it into its appropriate slot...but backing that HUMONGOUS van (it seemed so that first time for sure) around the curve of the driveway and down that damned l...o...n...g...hill seemed without end! But of course, we made it and were on our way. Me and Scott out on the highway even, in traffic...going somewhere, talk, talk, talking a mile a minute. There didn't seem enough time to say all we had to say to each other. Dinner was great, and then we got set to head home. First time I'd been away with Scott alone, "far from the maddening crowd..." naturally, afraid I'd forget something or afraid something would happen that I wouldn't know how to handle. (Folks, you've got to admit the fear...it's there; no need to act like it isn't...or just call it "nervous"; same thing! Later, you can laugh about it when you realize how silly you were...If you don't admit it, you get no reward of laughter afterward, no mental pat on the back!) And yes, I forgot something but remembered before we got back out on the highway; actually before we'd even pulled out of the parking lot.

I was depending on Scott to remind me (which he is usually very good at and patient (?) with...getting better at that in '97...but then, he's had a lot more practice by now, too). He and I were busy enjoying our outing, the talking so we both forgot to tie his chair down! Thankfully, I did remember and fixed...I can just imagine what might have happened if I'd looked back in the rearview mirror out on the highway and saw Scott's chair going who knows where! Worse case scenario being out the door and down the highway, weaving in and out of all the "race cars" out there trying to go faster than everyone else!

That worst case scenario always gets us through you know…Go ahead and figure it, prepare for it, think how you would handle everything. Get ready for it…Chances are it will never, ever happen so even if it is truly bad, it won't be "worst case," a piece of cake comparatively! Works…Try it…Practice it…You'll see.

I can't remember which trip but on one of the times when Roger and I both were in Illinois with Scott, we all went into St. Louis. All those times get so jumbled in my mind now…years later. One trip was after the bad flood in that area; Beth was with us also and Scott went by where he had been in rehab at the request of the staff, to visit with a "new spinal cord patient," a young girl. On another trip, we were at one of the malls and had gotten slices of pizza. Roger was being "too helpful" and making Scott uncomfortable. When Scott gets impatient with me, I may be uncomfortable and frustrated but try not to over-react. Scott told Roger he was a pain in the ass…and I immediately felt my nerves tightening up, but without missing a beat Roger just matter-of-factly said, "Sometimes you're a pain in the ass, too." Just like two normal brothers. This is a perfect example of how Roger has been with Scott since his accident. THERE for him, absolutely and with a sincerely open, loving heart but also honest and not accepting any bullshit. It's easy to get caught in that damned if you do, damned if you don't place…Roger's response to Scott's "criticism" broke the tenseness, and we all laughed AT/WITH each other. It was wonderful, and I heard the hope speaking in my mind that we all could learn to get through all our stresses and irritations this easily, with laughter being the end result.

On the other hand, I doubt that anyone is more concerned or upset if he feels Scott isn't treated with dignity or respect than Roger; if he hears an attendant saying something perhaps in fun which may detract from his brother's sense of self-esteem. He has been steadfast in his position as Scott's brother/Jim's son…and the mediation role practiced therein. He is well prepared because he loves them both.

In the fall, I made another trip to Greenville to visit with Scott…Roger and Beth came up, too, but we each drove our own vehicles. It was Roger's turn to have a dog story, but his wasn't funny. This time, Blade was gone but Scott now had a beautiful Rottweiler named Cain. Roger was playing with Cain; Cain was eating some M&M's off the floor…bad timing. Cain nipped Roger's chin. I had been in town, picking up something for Scott at the medical supply store…right across the street from Dr. Daisy's office. Called Scott to find out something, and he told me what had happened and that Roger and Beth were at Dr. Daisy's office. Sure enough, looked out the window and there was their car; so, after making my purchases, I went over to check them out. Roger had to have stitches, and the butterfly bandage they'd put over them just wouldn't stay stuck on his handsome face!

I think this trip was the time I was going to drive Scott into Highland for therapy…and we got poured on. Not so hard for me, I could easily change clothes but again, Rachel saved Scott from pneumonia by getting dry clothes back on him, dry shoes and socks.

When I got there, my niece Val who was also Scott's attendant (mornings/evenings) had planted beautiful flowers at the bottom of Scott's ramp by the driveway, but the weeds had grown up so badly that the flowers could hardly be seen. I tackled the weeding project and as I was doing so, Scott told me to watch out for the spider's web, not to damage it. Sure enough, there was this big "beautiful" black spider with yellow markings on its back. I knew Scott had spent hours watching that spider do her work in his flower garden, and I thanked her for her entertainment and carefully removed the weeds around her web, not destroying any more than I had to. The next morning, there was a magnificent web in all its newly spun glory among the flowers, dewdrops glistening on it like diamonds in the bright sunlight.

Later, back in Orlando, I found a spider made from wire and beads in one of my craft magazines. The first one I made was for Scott; he still has it hanging in his home in Lake Placid, Florida but that part of the story still awaits us. There is a story that accompanies the spider...aside from the spider in Scott's flower garden that motivated my new appreciation of large, black and yellow spiders at least. On Christmas Eve, a mother prepared for a visit from Christ. She cleaned, scrubbed and decorated the tree...spiders crept out to see it, crawled on the branches...leaving cobwebs behind them. Christ saw the webs and knew they would sadden the mother, so he turned the webs into ropes of gold and silver, making the tree even more beautiful. The spider in the garden was for Scott; the legend in the craft book was for me based on my newly acquired appreciation of spiders!

During the summer and early fall months of that year, aside from getting Scott's van modified so Scott could drive and getting a power chair (still on my list, at least), I was wanting something more personally satisfying for Scott. Rachel was still in his life, but there was a change. They both kept gaining a little more independence from each other; I was wanting Scott to meet someone NEW who would care about him in his new circumstances...just so Scott would know it could still be that way, not at all to hurt Rachel, so I didn't press it. Time went by...and it happened. When it did, I felt similar to how I'd felt when Scott told me he sometimes forgot he was in a wheelchair. After that, I felt he would again KNOW it could still be his choice if he wanted to attract someone's attention, that he could still "score" and could still decide yes or no as to how far he wanted to go with it.

IT was happening...We had learned so much...Together...Apart...We were still A Family. At the end of 1993, we didn't know how 1994 would be...but we were feeling pretty confident that it would be an even better year than 1993 had been, and that hadn't been so bad.

CHAPTER FIVE

Lake Placid, Florida's New Resident 1994

Lake Placid, Florida, is 100 miles +/- southwest of Orlando, about 20 miles south of Sebring where the races are held annually. It's a fairly rural community with beautiful lakes scattered throughout the area. Scott had lived in Lake Placid earlier in life when working in that area of Florida. I had often visited him there in times past.

By winter's end in Illinois, 1994, Scott's mind had mentally arranged a permanent move to Florida. Roger and I went to work checking out apartments; I have a large manila envelope full of responses to faxes I sent to apartment managers throughout the Orlando area. Instead of making calls, I made an inquiry sheet that asked about accessible apartments: availability, price, washer and dryer hook-ups, etc. I tried to get their definition of accessible because what others may consider accessible doesn't necessarily prove to be so.

Back in Illinois, preparations were being made for the move once an affordable apartment or place to live had been found and attendant care worked out, finances, etc. Rachel would drive Scott down in the van; and my A#1 big brother, Tuny (who else?), would help load up a U-Haul truck with everything from inside the trailer and drive it then to Florida. His son, Tom, would help him with the loading, unloading and driving. Scott's van had not been modified so he could drive, which meant he would still be dependent on others to drive him after he made the move. Rachel would remain in Greenville and continue with her schooling, no other family lived nearby; there were old friends who committed to "being there," but we knew in reality, they might or might not be. The intentions are totally pure; the reality demands recognition of requirements. Adjustments and shifting of plans occur, one's thinking and perceptions adapt; eventually things fall in place, but it takes time. Regardless, the intentions provided security support to Scott's plans. He was going to be some place, truly alone...but the "others" would be there if he needed them. We all welcomed that...but waited to see if it would work out that way.

Scott decided to move back to Lake Placid as rent was so much less there. This meant Roger, Beth and I wouldn't be nearby to help, to drop in often. We could visit and did, but we couldn't drop by for a cold drink with him, or to adjust the A/C or heat for him. He had friends there; so if it couldn't be Orlando, we were agreeable to Lake Placid. Medical services and the support group weren't as available, but choices always have to be weighed one against the other. This was Scott's choice. His life. We would support that.

By March, he had found a duplex there via Ma Bell. The price and space were right, but no one had seen it come moving day. His landlord had been agreeable to Scott's renovations as required for accessibility...so as my brother and nephew were driving the U-haul from Illinois, as I drove from Orlando to Lake Placid to meet the travelers (first the U-Haul, then Scott and Rachel in the van), and I'm sure as Scott and Rachel were heading south...we all were wondering what would have to be done to prepare for Scott's entry and residence in his new home. Jim hadn't thought he would be able to help with the move; but fortunately, he had some work to coordinate in the area so was available to help move Scott into his new home after all with tools in hand. As it turned out, it wasn't so bad; but ramps had to be built at the front door, then the back door that led out onto a screened in porch. Tuny, Jim and Tom played carpenter, etc. after they'd helped move everything in from the van. Small world sometimes...friends of my brother, Bud, in Jerseyville, Illinois, lived right across the street!

Scott's landlord's mother and her friend lived in the other half of the duplex, and they welcomed this swarm of new people warmly...went out of their way to make sure everything was all right for Scott; changed out the refrigerator so he would be able to open it. This is how they were the day he moved it; is how they have remained...except for health problems which have slowed down their own activities. They've been worth their weight in gold for the kindnesses and assistances given while Scott has lived next door to them.

What a day...Rachel stayed for a while beyond move-in day; then returned to Greenville. Scott was truly "on his own..." arranging his care, his life, paying his bills, all of it. At night, there was no roommate in another room; no one coming in during the night to check on him. An attendant would come in in the morning to get him up, help him with his hygiene and personal care and leave; at night, another would come in to put him to bed. His days and his nights were his own again. Almost three years after his accident...

As when he went to Normandy Manor, we waited...one night at a time to see if he was all right...the nights became weeks; the weeks became months...There have been times, it seemed he would be better off near Roger, Beth and myself; but those have been few, and once a "crisis" passed, Lake Placid continued to feel like the better location for him. Old friends were still there; new ones were found. His base kept expanding.

He is close enough, we get together fairly often. Far enough away, we don't all become too dependent on each other although at this point, that's less likely regardless. Scott knows how to cope and arrange things now; has more confidence in himself and less need to have a "companion" interfering in his life and comfortable routines. When he moved to Lake Placid, he still could not drive his van. That was an inconvenience...but he filled his hours, reading, TV, computer, pushing his chair for blocks and blocks. He still wasn't wanting to give up what he'd gained in strength from that by getting into a powerchair.

One day when we were talking on the phone, he told me about his adventure the night before. He'd run out of Skoal! It was dark, but he pushed himself up the street and around the corner to the little convenience store and got some on his own! I was proud of him, but it wasn't real safe for him to have done that! There was traffic, no sidewalk; he had no "lights." Roger and I both admired his spunk, regardless of the motivation...but thought we might have to get Scott headlights and tail-lights for his wheelchair if he was going to pull that kind of stuff!

June, 1995. The modifications to his van were nearing completion! During the last week of modifications, his van had to stay in the shop…about a hundred miles from Lake Placid. The final days, he would have to go over (get a driving service to take him) and be there for those final placements and adjustments. I went with him one day…what a long day: the ride over, the hours throughout the day, the ride back to Lake Placid; then for me, driving back to Orlando, but I very much wanted to be there, and it was reassuring to meet the manager and the staff doing the work. It was evident, they realized how important their work was and were sensitive to the needs of their clients. The cost for their expertise was high…and worth every penny of it, more even…If I hadn't already realized that, and I did, it would have become crystal clear as I saw Scott DRIVE the van out of the garage, taking it out onto a busy street for a test drive!!!!! What a beautiful sight, comparable only to when I saw him take his first STEPS as a baby…under the tree in Mom's front yard. He was gone for quite a while…then pulled back into the lot, backed it into the garage.

The next day, Roger took his turn and went back to the shop with Scott. He filmed the events of the day, and then rode home with Scott; this time, Scott doing the driving…taking his van home to park in his own driveway…No more waiting for someone else to come drive for him. Freedom.

My only concern at the beginning was that Scott didn't have a car phone…in case he had problems; but then, we got used to his coming and going at his leisure. Eventually, he got the phone which is better…but waiting for a phone didn't stop him; he'd waited too long to be behind the wheel again and wasn't going to let something like that stop him!

His first trip out of the Lake Placid area…he came to see me in Orlando. This time, as I write, there isn't laughter although there were certainly huge smiles upon his arrival at the time…Instead, there are these warm, thankful tears blearing the words before me on the screen of this computer…

The last time Scott had driven his own vehicle to my place was well before the accident…It took him then four years plus to do it again. It had been even longer than that since I had ridden in a vehicle with Scott driving. We enjoyed that pleasure again on the same day. I had a special friend here with me to greet Scott on that occasion. Shortly after I met this man…way before he met Scott, he was building a ramp onto the back of his house, just in case Scott ever wanted to come visit with him…he would be able to easily. Roger had not flinched for a second over any need for involvement in his brother's new circumstances since they first began. Beth being Beth was ready for whatever was needed…any time, any where, any way. I was in the midst of people with huge hearts…Scott's being one of the most fearless and determined. He'd had to give up his manual chair pretty much, as he couldn't drive in that; but I'm sure he felt being able to drive vs. being able to push his own chair was an equitable exchange! I, on the other hand, was relieved at the change from manual to power and purely thrilled to see him driving.

It has been fearful to realize that quadriplegics living independently yet still REQUIRING the presence of an attendant or home health aide to put them to bed, to get them up, dress them and do personal or medical procedures for them (routine or emergency)...once mobile (having a modified van which enables them to drive) may be perceived as less dependent on those requirements by the powers that be. Nothing but the perception has changed. The modified van is really no more than a glorified powerchair...or even a manual, push chair...and should not be an indication for less personal/medical care requirements. One may travel a bit further; but there still cannot be any overnight visits with friends or family. There should be awards for courage and determination and independence, not the threat of loss because the fight for increased independence has continued and has been successful. For those who may find themselves in this precarious position, I remember you in my prayers and hope our leaders may realize the huge difference that exists between perception and reality. YOU are our best EDUCATORS. OTHERS, those who provide or authorize approval for services and care, MUST LEARN. This is just one example of how ignorance exists in the able-bodied world beyond paralysis. The importance of each need becomes prime during times of extreme need, and there are so many needs.

Another frustration has been the tangle of approvals required, so usually ignored, relating to "Safety" approval for modified vehicles/transportation for those in wheelchairs. I have a specific example in mind: A consideration had been given for distribution of the "Elaine Anne Lift and Driving System." There is a fine gentleman in Canada whose daughter survived a spinal cord injury and is now also quadriplegic. This father, who also was an engineer, had a personal involvement in designing transportation for his daughter that was SAFE and reliable. The Elaine Anne Lift and Driving System is being manufactured and distributed in Canada with endless satisfaction for others in wheelchair.

He flew to Tampa, Florida, to meet with Scott. There was discussion of setting up a distributorship in the U.S. Others from the Department of Transportation who were there for another meeting, agreed to take "some" time to meet with Scott and Ken. Scott had managed to coordinate this meeting from his wheelchair via Ma Bell. He had the enthusiasm and the product and a personal interest in presenting it to the public. There are so many reasons why this system is FAR SUPERIOR and the technology beyond what is available here in the States; but there was absolutely no interest expressed or even encouragement given to promote future activity by those who could affect such actions. I wondered afterward why these "fine" gentlemen had even agreed to meet. They were only negative in their comments.

The tangle of inspections and approvals that would be required are to such an extent that the improved mode of transportation for those in wheelchairs was not even considered. Their attitude was what was presently available and had been approved was good enough. How would Scott, and others, even be alive today if that had been the attitude of those in the medical field who fought to find a way to improve the mortality rate of those who became paralyzed, and beyond that...to improve their extended lives then as paraplegics and quadriplegics. At such times, although I would not ordinarily want my worst enemy to endure quadriplegia for even one hour of their life, I cannot help but wish such "forces of power and authority" could...long enough to appreciate the need for action and interest. It is so obvious to those who are personally involved and is such a blind spot for those who are not. I understand that. This type of situation is beyond our normal realization of life's needs. It is frustrating because of my ignorance in how to teach those who do not care to learn.

A perfect example would have been provided as Scott and I were leaving the hotel where the meeting had been held. This was before Scott's van had been modified, so I had made the trip to Tampa with Scott from Lake Placid and served as his driver. The lift was malfunctioning enough to make me uncomfortable, and as Scott was trying to get into the van so we could return to Lake Placid, the lift kept trying to fold up WITH HIM ON IT. Thank God Ken was still with us, helping me make sure Scott got in safely. At one point, if he hadn't caught Scott with his arms and strength, Scott would have been thrown backward onto the floor of the van behind him. There would have been nothing I could have done to keep it from happening. I was so frightened but couldn't allow Scott to see how it had affected me; we still had the long drive back to Lake Placid ahead of us, and I didn't want Scott anymore stressed than he already was. Eventually, Scott got the "malfunction" found and fixed in the system, but it could happen again.

Now, he is alone…driving…If it would happen again, there would be no one THERE to help him, to keep it from happening. Yet, the "power forces" couldn't consider anything else…due to the safety factors and bureaucratic red tape that would come into play. Go Figure If You Can…I CAN'T and I live with the fear of such a reoccurrence.

When Scott's rehab progressed to the point he could use a fork with the aid of a cuff that fits onto his hand, we realized that a three-tined fork worked better; he could stab his food easier with the wider tines. Word was passed within the family to be on the look out for three-tined forks. I was having breakfast after church with my friends, Billie & Steve, at The Olive Garden one morning. Eureka! Wonderful forks…I asked the Manager if I could buy some and explained why I wanted them. He told me to take as many as I wanted and that I was welcome to come back at any time for more. (There are those who are sensitive after all.) A few weeks later, at a casual Christmas party for the office there was a large three-tined fork in the assorted collection of dinnerware. Someone made a funny remark about how anyone could eat with it…I didn't say anything while wishing I could take that magnificent fork home with me for Scott. It didn't seem appropriate to bring up our situation in the midst of a happy event.

There are hundreds of fears and frustrations as to why some procedures and methods MUST REMAIN as they presently are. Most can be "lived with" more easily than others; some, such as the need for attendant care regardless of mobility and the safety factors relating to approval of new/improved transportation and equipment, remain in need of major attention and change. There are ignorances which are justifiable as experience has not played a role in educating; there are ignorances which are inexcusable because a knowledge would affect such significant increases in accessibility and in maintenance of life. There have been such important improvements in the past twenty years; I must hope those improvements continue to double and triple in years to come and lead finally to a cure.

Tomorrow's date as I put the final lines onto this paper…will be June 29, 1997!

Another anniversary of the change in our lives…the sixth one this time.

THAT FIRST YEAR won't last forever…and you'll eventually find life turning around, progressing, building once more. While dealing with the trauma, give yourself time to adjust to the change, time to learn…Everything can't happen or be known at once. Trust time.

There will be a cure one day for spinal cord injuries. No one knows when yet, but it will happen. Scott has always hoped for that but has not waited for it. At the beginning, I couldn't think about a cure…I HAD TO DEAL WITH THE MOMENT. It seemed important to make sure Scott did that. When he would talk to me about a cure, I would tell him that was between him and God and that I trusted both but I was too busy dealing with right now, maybe a bit beyond that to the next day, maybe into next week. Scott was stronger than me. He could do both: look confidently toward the day when a cure would be found while learning how to live as fully as possible in the present.

With Scott getting his life once more under control, I find my mind is more open to the research being done. His confidence is contagious; I find myself believing more and more there will be a cure also.

Unfortunately/Fortunately we now have a loyal champion of the cause; one people everywhere know and respect so listen to. Of course, I mean Christopher Reeve. I know his personal tragedy will have an impact on everyone who finds himself/herself becoming intimately acquainted with transportation via wheelchair and all that accompanies their travels therein. We all salute his bravery, gallantry and determination. God Bless You and Yours, Dear Christopher…and thank you. Scott and I have gone through those initial weeks of "recovery" with you; remembering where he had been along the stages as your own private Hell Week and those that followed were endured. Your presence at the Academy Awards…we knew what a supreme effort that had to have taken, and we knew how much courage was shown in exposing yourself to the world during such a vulnerable time in your life. Scott was relating to you then as you did later to the young man experiencing his new life as a quadriplegic with his mother in their home during a show that I watched on TV. As I stated at the beginning of this writing, we are a family…those of us touched by this trauma. Many of us will remain strangers to each other, but we are family nonetheless.

We all have our "stories," Scott especially…Jim and Peggy, Roger and Beth, Rachel…Mine can't help but overflow into theirs; I realize that but have no intent to tell their stories. My intent throughout has been a re-creation of this mother's experience with a spinal cord injury that might serve to help others if they find themselves meeting the ghost behind the wheelchair of their beloved son or daughter. As Robin said, "It will get easier."

I would give honor and remembrance to Marty and Craig and Doug; also to their mothers and my friends, Shirley, Connie and Carolyn whose stories took them along other paths.

I would give honor and remembrance to Michael and Gay who began this story with me and are so much a part of its creation. I miss them. I miss our talks and our times together. I will treasure forevermore the gifts they left behind.

November 1, 1997. I have found there is another to be honored and remembered even more in these pages than when I thought this story had been told. On Sunday, October 26, 1997, my brother who has been mentioned so often and in such generous and loving ways, left us and has joined Michael and Gay. Among other things, this manuscript has been meant to be an expression of my appreciation for the blessing he has been in our lives. It is with such sadness…and with such Precious Memories that I add,"In Memory of Urban L. "Tuny" Ridings, September 2, 1930-October 26, 1997," who will always be missed and will always be thought of with love in our hearts.

Life is full of EVERYTHING…Celebrations and Times of Grief. A LIFE is as it is lived; it is not the length of that life that is the quantifier of its quality. Each Moment as it passes is Precious.

ABOUT THE AUTHOR

Lila Leona Ridings Darnell was born and raised in the rolling, wooded hills of Terrapin Ridge, a rural area outside of Greenville, Illinois. The youngest of eight children, she grew up just down the hill from the church she, her family and all the families of the other area homesteaders attended. At their late ages, her strict father and mother were a little softer on their baby girl than they'd been with her older siblings. Her father Urban Lee was a millwright in the steel mills of Granite City who loved reading and discussing the Bible and was a gifted writer, and her mother Beatrice cooked, sewed and quilted a wonderful if simple life for her family. "Lila Lee" was married in February, 1961, before graduating high-school in the spring of 1962. Her first son, Scott Alan, became the pride and joy of both of his parents and a large, loving family on September 23, 1963.

The young Darnell family traveled much in pursuit of work, settling briefly in Iowa and Florida in between return moves to Greenville. Along the way another son, Roger Kent, was born, on May 5, 1966. Having received the writing gift from her father, Lila learned to tap the well often as a means for dealing with life's joys, challenges and hardships. In 1974, she became a single-mother, raising two very active boys while navigating a career as an administrator and while learning of the unprotected world beyond marriage.

During the years when her boys were growing into men, her blood, sweat and tears were all set down in volumes of verses, many of which have been destroyed and buried along with the more difficult memories. What remains is a strong mother and an independent woman, who enjoys a special solace and strength every day from her knowledge of the two sons she helped to raise and the lives they've built from their bonds of love and experience.

Still compelled to write both fiction and verse, the writing of this book was yet another example of the way Ms. Ridings Darnell has used writing as a therapy throughout her life's journey. According to the feedback of the many readers who sat down with these pages as they came together, the words have now taken on a medicinal, healing life of their own, no doubt from the sincere desire of this devoted mother to not only make a difference for her son in a time of unimaginable difficulty, but to build hope for all the others who have been touched by the sudden, life-shattering arrival of a paralyzing injury.

Ms. Ridings Darnell lives, works and writes in Orlando, Florida.